HomeBuilders Parenting Series™

Raising
Children
of Faith

By Dennis and Barbara Rainey

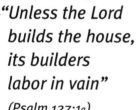

*"Unless the Lord
builds the house,
its builders
labor in vain"
(Psalm 127:1a).*

FAMILYLIFE™
Bringing Timeless Principles Home
Little Rock, Arkansas

Group
Loveland, Colorado

Group's R.E.A.L. Guarantee to you:

This Group resource incorporates our R.E.A.L. approach to ministry—one that encourages long-term retention and life transformation. It's ministry that's:

Relational
Because learner-to-learner interaction enhances learning and builds Christian friendships.

Experiential
Because what learners experience through discussion and action sticks with them up to 9 times longer than what they simply hear or read.

Applicable
Because the aim of Christian education is to equip learners to be both hearers and doers of God's Word.

Learner-based
Because learners understand and retain more when the learning process takes into consideration how they learn best.

Raising Children of Faith

Copyright © 2003 Dennis and Barbara Rainey

Visit our Web site: **www.grouppublishing.com**

Credits
FamilyLife
Editor: David Boehi

Group Publishing, Inc.
Editor: Matt Lockhart
Creative Development Editor: Paul Woods
Chief Creative Officer: Joani Schultz
Copy Editors: Lyndsay E. Gerwing and Alison Imbriaco
Art Directors: Jenette L. McEntire and Jean Bruns
Print Production Artists: Stephen Beer and Joyce Douglas
Cover Art Director: Jeff A. Storm
Cover Designer: Alan Furst, Inc.
Cover Photographer: Daniel Treat
Illustrator: Ken Jacobsen
Production Manager: Peggy Naylor

ISBN 0-7644-2544-7
10 9 8 7 6 5 4 3 2 1   12 11 10 09 08 07 06 05 04 03

Printed in the United States of America.

How to Let the Lord Build Your House
and not labor in vain

The HomeBuilders Parenting Series™: A small-group Bible study dedicated to making your family all that God intended.

FamilyLife is a division of Campus Crusade for Christ International, an evangelical Christian organization founded in 1951 by Bill Bright. FamilyLife was started in 1976 to help fulfill the Great Commission by strengthening marriages and families and then equipping them to go to the world with the gospel of Jesus Christ. The Weekend to Remember conference is held in most major cities throughout the United States and is one of the fastest-growing marriage conferences in America today. "FamilyLife Today," a daily radio program hosted by Dennis Rainey, is heard on hundreds of stations across the country. Information on all resources offered by FamilyLife may be obtained by contacting us at the address, telephone number, or World Wide Web site listed below.

Dennis Rainey, Executive Director
FamilyLife
P.O. Box 8220
Little Rock, AR 72221-8220
1-800-FL-TODAY
www.familylife.com

A division of Campus Crusade for Christ International
Bill Bright, Founder
Steve Douglass, President

About the Sessions

Each session in this study is composed of the following categories: Warm-Up, Blueprints, Wrap-Up, and HomeBuilders Project. A description of each of these categories follows:

Warm-Up (15 minutes)

 The purpose of Warm-Up is to help people unwind from a busy day and get to know each other better. Typically the first point in Warm-Up is an exercise that is meant to be fun while introducing the topic of the session. The ability to share in fun with others is important in building relationships. Another component of Warm-Up is the Project Report (except in Session One), which is designed to provide accountability for the HomeBuilders Project that is to be completed by couples between sessions.

Blueprints (60 minutes)

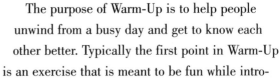 This is the heart of the study. In this part of each session, people answer questions related to the topic of study and look to God's Word for understanding. Some of the questions are to be answered by couples, in subgroups, or in the group at large. There are notes in the margin or instructions within a question that designate these groupings.

Wrap-Up (15 minutes)

 This category serves to "bring home the point" and wind down a session in an appropriate fashion.

HomeBuilders Project (60 minutes)

 This project is the unique application step in a HomeBuilders study. Before leaving each meeting, couples are encouraged to "Make a Date" to complete the project for the session prior to the next group meeting. Most HomeBuilders Projects contain three sections: (1) As a Couple—a brief exercise designed to get the date started; (2) Individually—a section of questions for husbands and wives to answer separately; and (3) Interact as a Couple—an opportunity for couples to share their answers with each other and to make application in their lives.

Another feature you will find in this course is a section of Parent-Child Interactions. There is a corresponding interaction for each session. These interactions provide parents an excellent opportunity to communicate with their children on the important topics covered in this course.

In addition to the above regular features, occasional activities are labeled "For Extra Impact." These are activities that generally provide a more active or visual way to make a particular point. Be mindful that people within a group have different learning styles. While most of what is presented is verbal, a visual or active exercise now and then helps engage more of the senses and appeals to people who learn best by seeing, touching, and doing.

About the Authors

Dennis Rainey is the executive director and the co-founder of FamilyLife (a division of Campus Crusade for Christ) and a graduate of Dallas Theological Seminary. Since 1976, he has overseen the rapid growth of FamilyLife's conferences and resources. He began the HomeBuilders Couples Series and the HomeBuilders Parenting Series and is also the daily host of the nationally syndicated radio program "FamilyLife Today."

Dennis and his wife, Barbara, have spoken at FamilyLife conferences across the United States and overseas. Dennis is also a speaker for Promise Keepers. He has testified on family issues before Congress and has appeared on numerous radio and television programs.

Dennis and Barbara have co-authored several books, including *Building Your Mate's Self-Esteem* (re-released as *The New Building Your Mate's Self-Esteem*), *Moments Together for Couples*, *Parenting Today's Adolescent*, and *Starting Your Marriage Right*.

Dennis and Barbara have served on the staff of Campus Crusade since 1971. They have six children and a growing number of grandchildren. They are both graduates of the University of Arkansas and live near Little Rock, Arkansas.

Contents

Acknowledgments **8**

Introduction **9**

Session One: Your Job as a Parent......................................**13**

Session Two: Introducing Your Children to God.................**25**

Session Three: Helping Your Children Walk With God.......**39**

Session Four: Building Character in Your Children.............**53**

Session Five: Training Your Children to Love Others **67**

Session Six: Imparting a Sense of Purpose **81**

Parent-Child Interactions.......................................**93**

Where Do You Go From Here?...**109**

Our Problems, God's Answers **113**

Leaders Notes..**123**

Recommended Resources...**150**

Acknowledgments

You could say that this study has taken us a lifetime to put together. Any time we develop material on the subject of parenting, we draw from everything we've learned over the years—from our own parents, from the Scriptures, from books, from outstanding teachers, and from our experience raising six children. And we're still learning.

We first want to thank our colleagues at FamilyLife from over the years who worked with us to develop this content, which is based largely on principles from the FamilyLife Parenting Conference. It is such a privilege to serve God with you.

A special word of thanks goes to Dave Boehi, who is a world-class homebuilder! With more than twenty-five years of ministry under his belt, he is an invaluable asset in a world-wide family reformation. Thanks, Dave, for the leadership and tender loving care you have given to this study and to the other HomeBuilders courses.

Group Publishing is a great partner for this series, and we appreciate the effort its editors make to ensure that every study helps create a unique and dynamic small-group learning experience. We especially want to acknowledge Matt Lockhart for his sensitive and creative work as the primary Group editor for all the HomeBuilders studies.

Finally, we would like to thank our own children for putting up with us as we've developed as parents! More than anyone else, they know we are not perfect parents. But as we have sought to build our family according to biblical principles, we have been pleased to see each child mature in a relationship with God. To paraphrase 3 John 4, we have no greater joy than to hear that our children are walking in the truth.

Introduction

Nearly all of the important jobs in our culture require intensive training. We would not think of allowing someone to practice medicine, for example, without first attending medical school and completing his or her residency.

But do you realize that most people receive little training in how to fulfill one of the most important responsibilities of our lives—being effective parents? When we bring a new life into the world, we burst with pride and joy...but are often ignorant about how to actually raise that child to become a mature, responsible adult.

In response to the need we see in families today, FamilyLife and Group Publishing have developed a series of small-group studies called the HomeBuilders Parenting Series. These studies focus on raising children and are written so that parents of children of all ages will benefit.

For these HomeBuilders studies, we have several goals in mind: First, *we want to encourage you in the process of child rearing.* We feel that being a mom or a dad is a high calling and an incredible privilege. We also know how easy it is to feel overwhelmed by the responsibility, especially when you have young children. Participating in a HomeBuilders group can connect you with other parents who share your struggles. The help and encouragement you receive from them will be invaluable.

Second, *we want to help you develop a practical, biblical plan for parenting.* It's so easy for parents to take parenting one day at a time. But as we've raised our six children, we've learned that we need to understand biblical guidelines on parenting and then make proactive plans to apply them.

Third, *we want to enhance and strengthen your teamwork as a couple*. You will learn together how to apply key biblical truths, and in the HomeBuilders Projects, you will talk through how to apply them to your unique family situation. In the process, you will have the opportunity to discuss issues that you may have ignored or avoided in the past. And you'll spend time regularly in prayer, asking God for his direction and power.

Fourth, *we want to help you connect with other parents so you can encourage and help one another.* You could complete this study with just your spouse, but we strongly urge you to either form or join a group of couples studying this material. You will find that the questions in each study will help create a special environment of warmth, encouragement, and fellowship as you meet together to learn how to build the type of home you desire. You will have the opportunity to talk with other parents to learn some new ideas...or to get their advice...or just to see that others are going through the same experiences. Participating in a HomeBuilders group could be one of the highlights of your life.

Finally, *we want to help you strengthen your relationship with God.* Not only does our loving Father provide biblical princi-ples for parenting, our relationship with him allows us to rely on his strength and wisdom. In fact, it is when we feel most powerless and inadequate as parents that he is most real to us. God loves to help the helpless parent.

The Bible: Blueprints for Building Your Family

You will notice as you proceed through this study that the Bible is used frequently as the final authority on issues of life, marriage, and parenting. Although it was written thousands of years ago, this Book still speaks clearly and powerfully about the struggles we face in our families. The Bible is God's Word—his blueprints for building a God-honoring home and for dealing with the practical issues of living.

We encourage you to have a Bible with you for each session. For this series we use the New International Version as our primary reference. Another excellent translation is the New American Standard Bible.

A Special Word to Single Parents

Although the primary audience for this study is married couples, we recognize that single parents will benefit greatly from the experience. If you are a single parent, you will find that some of the language and material does not apply directly to you. But most of what you will find in this study is timeless wisdom taken directly from Scripture that can help you develop a solid, workable plan for your family. We hope you will be flexible and adapt the material to your specific situation.

If possible, you might want to attend the group sessions with another single parent. This will allow you to encourage each other and hold each other accountable to complete the HomeBuilders Projects.

Ground Rules

Each group is designed to be enjoyable and informative— and nonthreatening. Three simple ground rules will help ensure that everyone feels comfortable and gets the most out of the experience.

1. Don't share anything that would embarrass your spouse or violate the trust of your children.

2. You may pass on any question you don't want to answer.

3. If possible, plan to complete the HomeBuilders Project as a couple between group sessions.

A Few Quick Notes About Leading a HomeBuilders Group

1. Leading a group is much easier than you may think! A group leader in a HomeBuilders session is really a "facilitator." As a facilitator, your goal is simply to guide the group through the discussion questions. You don't need to teach the material—in fact, we don't want you to! The special dynamic of a HomeBuilders group is that couples teach themselves.

2. This material is designed to be used in a home study, but it also can be adapted for use in a Sunday school environment. (See page 125 for more information about this option.)

3. We have included a section of Leaders Notes in the back of this book. Be sure to read through these notes before leading a session; they will help you prepare.

4. For more material on leading a HomeBuilders group, get a copy of the *HomeBuilders Leader Guide*, by Drew and Kit Coons. This book is an excellent resource that provides helpful guidelines on how to start a study, how to keep discussion moving, and much more.

Your Job as a Parent

We need to look to God and the Bible to discover the values we need to pass on to our children.

W A R M • U P   15   M I N U T E S

Getting Started

Introduce yourself, and share the names and ages of your children. Then respond to one or two of the following questions:

- If you were limited to three words to describe one of your children, what words would you choose?

- If you were to use just three words to describe yourself as a child, what words come to mind?

- What is one thing you hope to gain from this study?

Getting Connected

Pass your books around the room, and have couples

write in their names, phone numbers, and e-mail addresses.

_____
NAME, PHONE, AND E-MAIL

_____
NAME, PHONE, AND E-MAIL

_____
NAME, PHONE, AND E-MAIL

_____
NAME, PHONE, AND E-MAIL

_____
NAME, PHONE, AND E-MAIL

_____
NAME, PHONE, AND E-MAIL

BLUEPRINTS   60 MINUTES

Our Need for Direction

If you have a large group, form smaller groups of about six people to answer the Blueprints questions. Unless otherwise noted, answer the questions in your subgroup. Before moving into the Wrap-Up section, have subgroups report to the whole group the highlights from their discussion.

1. How well-prepared do you feel you were to become a parent? Rate yourself on the following scale, and explain why you ranked yourself where you did.

Poorly prepared   **Thoroughly prepared**

1   2   3   4   5   6   7   8   9   10

2. What is one thing you know about parenting now that you wish you had known when you first became a parent?

3. What would you say are the biggest challenges you face as a parent?

Raising "Successful" Children

One reason we can easily feel overwhelmed as parents is that the responsibility seems so difficult and complex in today's culture.

4. Consider the "typical" family in your community. What types of goals and dreams do you think the parents want to pass on to their children? What values do you think those goals and dreams represent?

5. Many parents go to a lot of effort and personal sacrifice to involve their children in a number of extracurricular activities (athletic teams, music lessons, swimming, ballet, and scouting to name several). Why do you think this is? What is the driving motivation?

6. What do you think many parents might miss in their desire to raise children who will be "successful"?

7. Think for a minute about your children and their future:

Answer question 7 with your spouse. After answering, you may want to share an appropriate insight or discovery with the group.

- What are one or two specific goals or dreams you have for your children that you hope they achieve by the time they are your age?

- What type of life do you desire for your children?

- What type of people do you pray your children will become?

Biblical Family Values

In the Bible we find a different set of values than we find in our culture.

8. Read Psalm 78:1-8 and Deuteronomy 6:1-7, answering the following questions for each:

- What does this passage say about biblical responsibilities for a parent?

- What does this passage say are the most important values a parent should pass on to a child?

	Responsibilities	*Values*
Psalm 78:1-8:		
Deuteronomy 6:1-7:		

9. In what ways do children benefit if they are raised to love God with all their heart, soul, and strength?

10. What impact do you imagine loving God "with all your heart...soul...and strength" can have on one's life, job, and family?

> **HomeBuilders Principle:**
> *As parents, we've been given the responsibility for telling our children about God and about their need to read and obey God's Word.*

Looking Ahead

In this session we've talked about the "big picture"—your job as a parent. But what does this mean, practically? To answer this question, we will look in the upcoming sessions at how your responsibility as parents is fulfilled in several critical areas:

* introducing your children to God,
* helping your children walk with God,
* building character in your children,
* training your children to love others, and
* imparting a sense of purpose.

Parenting Mission Statement

Based on what we have studied so far, what would
you say is the primary mission or responsibility of a
parent? Working with your spouse, spend several
minutes writing a one or two sentence parenting
mission statement. (There's a good chance you won't
finish crafting your statement in such a short time. Do
as much as you can, and plan to finish it during the
HomeBuilders Project you'll complete before the next
group session.) Then share your description with the
group. Take notes of ideas you can incorporate in
your own statement when you finish it during the
HomeBuilders Project.

After sharing your parenting mission statements, close this session in prayer. (Note: Starting on page 153, there are pages to record prayer requests.)

Make a Date

Make a date with your spouse to meet before the next session to complete the HomeBuilders Project. Your leader will ask at the next session for you to share one aspect of this experience.

DATE

TIME

LOCATION

HOMEBUILDERS PROJECT   6 0   M I N U T E S

As a Couple [10 minutes]

To start this project, reminisce about the day your first child arrived.

- What was the weather like that day?
- Who was the first person you told about the arrival of your child?

- Who were the first visitors to see your child?
- Who did people tell you your child looked like?
- What memory do you cherish the most from that day?

Individually [20 minutes]

1. What is one way you were challenged by the first session of this course?

2. As you look at your own family background, in what ways did your upbringing help prepare you to become a parent yourself? In what ways was your upbringing a negative influence on your preparation to become a parent?

3. What are your three greatest needs as a parent right now?

4. In what way or ways does your spouse help make you a better parent?

5. Up to this point, what would you say your top one or two goals for your children have been?

6. Read Psalm 78:1-8 and Deuteronomy 6:1-7. How would you evaluate the goals you identified in the previous question in light of what these passages say about the responsibilities of a parent?

7. Looking at your life up to this point, how would your children describe you? Write down how you think they would describe your life, your values, and your relationship with them.

8. Now write down some thoughts on how you would *like* your children to describe your life, your values, and your relationship with them.

Interact as a Couple [30 minutes]

1. Discuss your answers to the questions from the individual section.

2. Talk about the type of legacy you would like to leave your children. Also, if you weren't able to finish your parenting mission statement during the session, work to complete it.

3. Read through the following personal pledge:

I pledge to work with you to complete the Home-Builders Project after each session of this parenting study. I'll work to maintain an open attitude and not be defensive. If we do not complete all of each project, I will commit to doing so as soon as possible. I realize this process may be difficult at times, but our marriage and children are worthy of this investment.

(signed) _____

Will you honor your spouse by making this commitment? If so, sign this pledge in your spouse's book.

4. One of the greatest things you can do to ensure success in parenting is to pray. Ask God to give you the wisdom you need and to work in the life of your children. Thank the Lord for your children and for blessing you with the responsibility and privilege of parenthood. Pray for God's help in teaching, guiding, and training your children.

Be sure to check out the related Parent-Child Interaction on page 94.

Introducing Your Children to God

Children need to understand the basics of who God is and how to establish a relationship with him.

W A R M • U P   15   M I N U T E S

Your Spiritual Heritage

Whether or not your parents were religious, you learned something about God from them. Begin this session by talking about your spiritual upbringing:

- What was the spiritual environment in the home in which you grew up?

- What kind of spiritual influence have your parents had on you?

- Based on your spiritual background, how equipped do you feel to tell your children about God and how to have a relationship with him?

Project Report

Share one thing you learned from last session's HomeBuilders Project.

BLUEPRINTS   60 MINUTES

Our research at FamilyLife conferences has shown that the most important needs expressed by parents are

- knowing how to help their children come to know God personally and

- knowing how to help their children walk with God as they grow into adults.

In this session we will address the first need, and then we'll focus on the second need in Session Three.

Who's Responsible?

As we consider the need for our children to know God, one of the major decisions parents need to make is how involved they will be in this area of their children's lives.

Case Study

Bryce and Sherry have worked hard to build a solid life for their family. Bryce sells commercial real estate, and Sherry works part time selling cosmetics from home. They have three daughters, ages thirteen, nine, and six. Life is typically busy for this family, and they feel the usual stress of keeping up with work, school, church, and various extracurricular activities.

While both Bryce and Sherry grew up going to church, they drifted away once they began attending college. About a year ago, they began attending a local church because they sensed that something was missing in their lives and they felt that some type of religious instruction should be part of their daughters' upbringing. They were also a bit concerned about their oldest daughter, who was developing a rebellious attitude. They were not pleased with some of her friends from school, and they hoped that she would encounter a more positive influence from the Christian kids at church.

Bryce and Sherry are excited about what they are learning from the Bible at their new church, but they feel awkward about discussing spiritual things in their home. They hear other parents at church talking about "family nights" in which they study the Bible with their children, but in their home they hardly ever talk about God, the Bible, or spiritual things.

After one "failed" attempt at a family night, Bryce and Sherry decided that they will let their church handle the religious instruction for their daughters, and they will handle the rest. "I don't have time to do everything," Bryce says. "Besides, isn't that what the church is for?"

If you have a large group, form smaller groups of about six people to answer the Blueprints questions. Unless otherwise noted, answer the questions in your subgroup. Before moving into the Wrap-Up section, have subgroups report to the whole group the highlights from their discussion.

1. Do you agree or disagree with the decision Bryce and Sherry made? Explain.

2. What has your experience been in grappling with spiritual training for your children?

3. Why do you think many parents delegate the responsibility for spiritual development to the church? How can this be detrimental or even counterproductive?

4. What do the following passages tell us about the power of parents to influence the faith of their children through their example and teaching?

- Deuteronomy 4:9-10

- Proverbs 22:4-6

- 2 Timothy 1:5

- 2 Timothy 3:14-15

Understanding and Responding to God

In Matthew 22:37-38, Jesus says that the "first and greatest commandment" is to "Love the Lord your God with all your heart and with all your soul and with all your mind." For us as parents, the first step in helping our children live by this commandment is to introduce them to God and help them establish a relationship with him.

An important part of this process is to help your children discover the answers to some basic questions about God.

Who Is God?

5. As a child, what type of picture did you have of God in your mind?

6. With each couple selecting one or more of the following passages, read your verses with your spouse, and answer the questions that follow for each passage you selected.

- Exodus 15:11
- Psalm 139:1-4
- Psalm 24:8-9
- Lamentations 3:22-23
- Psalm 33:6-11
- 1 John 4:8-10

- What do the verses you looked at tell us about God? (Try to communicate this concept in one or two sentences and in a way a young child could understand.)

- Why is it important in today's culture for our children to understand the character quality or qualities you identified in the verses you looked at?

After everyone has answered the preceding two questions, share your insights.

What kind of relationship does God desire with us?

7. Read Psalm 16:11 and John 10:10. What do these

verses tell us about the kind of relationship God desires with us?

What stands between us and a relationship with God?

8. Read Romans 3:10-12, 23. According to these verses, what separates us from God? Why would this separate us from God?

9. One of the ways you can tell your children what it means to be separated from God is to tell them about your own life. What was your life like when you were separated from God by your sin?

What is the solution to our problem?

10. According to John 14:6 and Romans 5:8, what did God do to make it possible for us to know him?

How should we respond?

11. What do John 1:12 and Ephesians 2:5-9 say about how we receive God's gift of salvation through Christ?

12. How did you come to understand the love of God as demonstrated in Christ?

W R A P • U P   15 M I N U T E S

Childlike Faith

Before closing this session in prayer, look at these two questions, sharing with the group if you are comfortable doing so.

- What are some ways you have taught your children about God and about how to establish a relationship with him?

- Have you had the opportunity to talk to a child about making a faith commitment to Christ? If so, tell the group about what happened.

Make a Date

Make a date with your spouse to meet before the next session to complete the HomeBuilders Project. Your leader will ask at the next session for you to share one aspect of this experience.

DATE

TIME

LOCATION

HOMEBUILDERS PROJECT   6 0   M I N U T E S

As a Couple [10 minutes]

From the list that follows, rank these items from 1 to 4, with 1 representing what you feel is your area of

---

greatest spiritual need as a parent.

___ I need more knowledge of who God is.

___ I need practical training on how to tell my child about God.

___ I need some age-specific resources that teach children about God.

___ I need accountability to an individual or to a group to begin to establish time to teach my child about God.

Discuss what you identified as your top need and why.

Individually [20 minutes]

1. What new or renewed insight did you gain from this session?

2. How well do you feel you have assumed the responsibility of teaching your children about God?

3. In what ways do you feel inadequate in your ability to be a spiritual mentor to your children?

4. What could you do as an individual to improve in this area? as a couple?

5. Read John 3:1-8. How confident are you that, in the words of Jesus, you are "born again"?

- ❏ absolutely certain
- ❏ fairly confident
- ❏ not certain at all
- ❏ don't really understand the concept

If you have doubts about whether you have personally established the type of relationship with God that we have discussed in this session, we have two suggestions:

- • Read the article "Our Problems, God's Answers," starting on page 113. This article provides more information about how to know God personally.

• Talk to your HomeBuilders group leader about what it means to be a Christian.

6. Put a plus **(+)** by each area that you think is a strength for your children and a minus **(-)** by each area that you think is a current need. If you don't think a statement applies at this time, leave that line blank.

Child: Child: Child:

____   ____   ____   understands who God is.

____   ____   ____   understands who Jesus Christ is.

____   ____   ____   is receptive to spiritual truths.

____   ____   ____   understands what sin is.

____   ____   ____   understands what forgiveness is.

____   ____   ____   understands why Christ died on the cross.

____   ____   ____   understands how to become a Christian.

____   ____   ____   has made a faith commitment to Christ.

7. What would you say are your children's greatest spiritual strengths? their greatest spiritual needs?

Interact as a Couple [30 minutes]

1. Review your answers from the individual section.

2. Assess where you feel each of your children is in relationship to God.

3. Discuss what you need to do to become better equipped to carry out your responsibility for the spiritual training of your children. Decide on one or two steps you will take.

4. End this time with prayer. Ask God to give you wisdom as you teach your children about God and how they can have a relationship with him.

Be sure to check out the related Parent-Child Interaction on page 96.

Helping Your Children Walk With God

Children need to learn from your example and teaching what it means to walk with God.

W A R M • U P   15   M I N U T E S

Dear Abby

Start this session by taking a couple of minutes to answer the following two questions individually:

For this activity everyone will need two index cards or two pieces of paper.

- If you could ask this group for advice on just one thing about training children, what would it be? Write your question on one of the index cards or pieces of paper.

- What parenting issue or concern related to your children are you dealing with? If you were to state this as a prayer request, what would it be? Write your request on the other index card or piece of paper.

When you're done, turn in your question and prayer request to the leader if you're comfortable doing so.

For this Warm-Up and, time permitting, during the regular closing prayer for this and the remaining sessions, your leader will randomly select one or two cards to read to the group. For questions, take a few minutes for group members to offer advice they might have. If you have experience with an issue someone has raised, relate to the group what was helpful to you in that situation. For prayer requests, spend a few minutes praying specifically for each request.

Project Report

Share one thing you learned from last session's HomeBuilders Project.

BLUEPRINTS   60 MINUTES

Mere Christianity

Once our children have made a decision to have a personal relationship with Christ, it is our responsibility as parents to help them grow in their faith.

1. What do you think it means to be a follower of Christ—a committed Christian?

If you have a large group, form smaller groups of about six people to answer the Blueprints questions. Unless otherwise noted, answer the questions in your subgroup. Before moving into the Wrap-Up section, have subgroups report to the whole group the highlights from their discussion.

2. What insights do the following passages give us into what our children need to know about being a Christian?

- Deuteronomy 10:12-13

- Ecclesiastes 12:13

- Micah 6:8

- Matthew 22:35-38

3. Would you be satisfied if your children grow to adopt the same type of relationship with God that you have? Why or why not?

FROG
Fully Rely on God

A Spiritual Greenhouse

4. What makes the home an ideal environment for providing spiritual training for children?

5. Read Deuteronomy 6:5-9. What does this passage tell us about how we as parents are to pass on biblical values to our children? What type of environment is needed to fulfill this responsibility?

6. What is likely to happen in a home in which biblical principles are formally taught but not lived out or modeled by the parents?

7. What is likely to happen in a home in which biblical principles are modeled but not formally taught?

8. How would you evaluate the spiritual training environment in your home? What are some specific things you have done in your home to create an environment in which your children are encouraged to grow in their knowledge of God?

Answer question 8 with your spouse. After answering, you may want to share an appropriate insight or discovery with the group.

HomeBuilders Principle:
The home should be a spiritual greenhouse where parents teach and model to their children how to walk with God.

Getting Practical

9. Read Psalm 78:1-8. What instruction do you find in this passage on what parents should teach and model to their children about walking with God?

10. One of the major exhortations to parents in Psalm 78 is found in verse 4, which speaks of telling "the next generation the praiseworthy deeds of the Lord, his power, and the wonders he has done."

- What is something praiseworthy God has done in your life that you could share with your child?

- Why do you think it's important for your child to hear you tell about the "praiseworthy deeds of the Lord" in your life?

11. Psalm 78 also tells of the command to parents "teach their children" (verse 5) in order that "they would put their trust in God" and "keep his commands" (verse 7). How would you teach your child to trust and obey God's commands if he or she

- was often caught telling lies?

- continually fought with siblings over what television shows to watch?

Faith Reflections

Reflect silently and individually for a few minutes on these questions:

- What is one way you've recently exercised faith and put your trust in God that you could share with your children?

- What is one way you've recently been obedient to God that you could share with your children?

Plan to share these examples of faith with your children this week.

As part of this session's closing prayer time, read prayer request cards from this session's Warm-Up time, and pray for as many of the requests as time permits. Requests or questions not covered in this session should be kept and addressed during the prayer or Warm-Up time in future sessions.

Make a Date

Make a date with your spouse to meet before the next session to complete the HomeBuilders Project.

DATE

_____

TIME

_____

LOCATION

HOMEBUILDERS PROJECT   6 0   M I N U T E S

As a Couple [10 minutes]

Start this date by answering these questions:

- Who has taught you the most about what it means to follow Jesus?
- How did this person teach you?

Take a few minutes to write in your book a short note of thanks and appreciation for what that person has done.

If your faith hero is still living, plan to communicate your appreciation to this person sometime over the next week.

Individually [20 minutes]

1. What did this session reveal to you—good or bad—about how you are doing in modeling and teaching your children to walk with God?

Evaluating Yourself as a Model and Teacher

2. Put a plus **(+)** by each area that you think is a strength for you and a minus **(-)** by each area that you think is a current need.

___ I have made a personal faith commitment to Christ.

___ I regularly spend time reading the Bible.

___ I am growing in my understanding and application of biblical principles.

___ I am growing in my understanding of the Holy Spirit.

___ I have a deep love and reverence for God.

___ I want to serve God as a demonstration of my faith.

___ I have a hunger for righteousness and the things of God.

___ I understand the value of prayer and pray regularly.

___ I am able to explain scriptural truths to others.

___ I view life through God's agenda—the Great Commandment (Matthew 22:36-38) and the Great Commission (Matthew 28:18-20).

___ I have a concern for telling others about Christ.

___ I share the message of Jesus with others.

___ I believe in the reliability and authority of Scripture.

___ I have taken a stand publicly for God.

___ I am growing closer to God.

___ I am involved in a church.

___ I am in fellowship with other Christians.

3. What are your top two spiritual strengths and needs?

Strengths	*Needs*

4. What spiritual commitment or re-commitment do you need to make as a result of this evaluation? Why not make that commitment right now and write it down? (If you are uncertain about your commitment to Christ, you may want to read the article "Our Problems, God's Answers," starting on page 113.)

Evaluating Your Child

5. Put a plus **(+)** by each area that you think is a strength for your children and a minus **(-)** by each area that you think is a current need. If you don't think the statement applies to your child at this time, leave it blank.

Child: Child: Child:

____   ____   ____ has made a personal commitment to Christ.

____   ____   ____ spends time reading the Bible.

____   ____   ____ is growing in understanding and application of biblical principles.

____   ____   ____ is growing in understanding of the Holy Spirit.

____   ____   ____ has a deep love and reverence for God.

____   ____   ____ has demonstrated a genuine faith.

____   ____   ____ has a hunger for righteousness and the things of God.

____	____	____	understands the value of prayer and prays regularly.
		____	is able to explain biblical truths to others.
____	____	____	views life through God's agenda—the Great Commandment and the Great Commission.
____	____	____	has a concern for telling others about Christ.
____	____	____	shares the message of Jesus with others.
____	____	____	believes in the reliability and authority of Scripture.
____	____	____	has taken a stand publicly for God.
____	____	____	is growing closer to God.
____	____	____	is involved in a church.
____	____	____	has Christian friends.

6. As you look over the evaluation you just completed, what do you think are your children's greatest strengths and needs?

	Child:	*Child:*	*Child:*
NEEDS			
STRENGTHS			

Interact as a Couple [30 minutes]

1. Talk through your answers to the questions from the individual section.

2. Agree on two action steps that you can take to help your children grow in their walk with God over the next year.

	Child: _____	*Child:* _____	*Child:* _____
ACTION STEP 1			
ACTION STEP 2			

3. Close your time by praying specifically for each of your children. Ask God to work through you to encourage their spiritual growth.

Be sure to check out the related Parent-Child Interaction on page 98.

Building Character in Your Children

Just as your children need training in everyday living skills, they also need training in character.

W A R M • U P   15   M I N U T E S

Character Traits

In the following list of character traits, circle three you think are especially important for your children to exhibit.

trustworthy	humble	teachable
obedient	kind	content
respectful	self-controlled	hopeful
loving	cooperative	faithful
honest	joyful	generous
courageous	patient	forgiving

After everyone has made selections, discuss what characteristics you chose and why.

Project Report

Share one thing you learned from last session's HomeBuilders Project.

BLUEPRINTS — 60 MINUTES

Response-ability

We define character as "response-ability." It's the ability to respond rightly to authority and to the challenges we face in life. Each day, we are faced with choices that test, refine, and reveal our character. We are tested in how we respond to life's circumstances—to the things mostly beyond our control that may cause irritation, anger, or annoyance. We are tested in how we respond to the different authorities in our lives and to the temptations and philosophies of the world. We are tested in how we respond to others, especially in times of conflict or when we don't get our own way. And we are tested during the hardships and trials of life.

RAISING CHILDREN OF FAITH

Case Study

As one of the top-ranked fourteen-year-old tennis players in the state, your son Jonathan is one of the favorites to win a weekend tournament. During the first day, he has little trouble defeating two opponents, but you are a bit disturbed by the attitude he displays on the court. When he misses a serve or makes a poor shot, he talks loudly to himself and hits the court with his racket.

The next day things get worse. First, a thunderstorm delays play, leaving your son with little to do for three hours. When his match finally begins, he is aggravated and impatient and makes several errors. His opponent is not nearly as skilled but manages to stay ahead during much of the match. As Jonathan fights to come back, he begins taunting his opponent and shouting at the referee to argue calls he doesn't agree with. As you look around the stands, it's hard not to notice that several parents are disturbed by Jonathan's behavior.

If you have a large group, form smaller groups of about six people to answer the Blueprints questions. Unless otherwise noted, answer the questions in your subgroup. Before moving into the Wrap-Up section, have subgroups report to the whole group the highlights from their discussion.

1. What do Jonathan's actions on the tennis court reveal about his need for character development? Describe his "response-ability"—his response to authority and to life's circumstances.

2. What are some different ways you could take action as Jonathan's parent in this situation?

HomeBuilders Principle:
Character is response-ability—
the ability to respond rightly to the challenges
we face in life.

The Attack on Character

Isaiah 53:6a tell us, "We all, like sheep, have gone astray, each of us has turned to his own way." Today, our culture increasingly encourages us to make our own choices about what is right or wrong and about how we should behave toward others. But true biblical character must be rooted in Scripture and in a relationship of trust and dependence upon God. Your goal as a parent is to point your children to a relationship with God in which they turn away from selfish desires and sin and live in obedience to God.

3. In what ways has our culture today made building character in a child more challenging than it was for your parents when they raised you?

4. In what specific ways have you seen your children's selfishness having an impact on their "response-ability"? How do they generally respond to authority? to difficult circumstances?

Character-Building Principles

5. Read 2 Timothy 3:14-17. What principles do you find in this passage that you can use in your home to build your child's character?

This passage from 2 Timothy has been the inspiration for a simple training process we've developed as we've worked with our own children. Following are four essential principles we use as a foundation for building a child's character:

- You build character by teaching your children the Scriptures.
- You build character by implementing a consistent system of discipline and rewards.
- You build character by continually training your children in the right way to live.
- You build character through your relationship with your children.

You build character by teaching your children the Scriptures.

6. What do the following Scriptures tell us about how your children will benefit from learning the truth of God's Word?

- Proverbs 2:1-15

- Proverbs 3:21-26

- Proverbs 6:20-23

You build character by implementing a consistent system of discipline and rewards.

7. As parents we are given the responsibility to address and confront our children's selfishness and wrong choices. Read Proverbs 5:23 and 10:17. What do you think will happen to your children if you fail to instruct, reprove, and correct them?

8. What are some examples of different ways to discipline a child?

9. Read Proverbs 15:23 and 16:24. Why is it important

that you offer praise, encouragement, and appropriate rewards to your children when they make right choices?

You build character by continually training your children in the right way to live.

As a parent, you train your children not only in the practical skills of everyday living, but also in *how* to live.

10. Let's say you have two young children, ages four and six, who don't play together well. They don't share their toys, they argue over who is in charge, and their method of resolving conflict is to scream at each other, hit each other, and call for you to settle the dispute.

- What type of training do they need?

- What character qualities do you need to build in them?

11. A critical component in your training program is your role as a model; no matter what you say to your children, your example will speak much louder. With your spouse, choose one of the following scenarios to discuss and then report back to the group. Work together to formulate a response to this question: What would you say to a parent who

- tells his or her children not to watch R-rated movies but often rents them to watch after the kids are in bed?

- disciplines his or her children for cheating or lying but doesn't tell the truth about the kids' ages in order to get a better price at the movies or a restaurant?

- does not allow his or her children to curse but loses control of his or her tongue when angry and uses obscenities?

You build character through your relationship with your children.

12. As you build character in your children, it is necessary to set rules and boundaries for them in different areas. What can happen, however, when parents overemphasize rules and do not build a warm, loving relationship with their children?

HomeBuilders Principle:
Building character in your children requires a commitment to teaching and training them to make wise, biblical choices.

Tennis Trouble Revisited

Look again at the Case Study (page 55) about
Jonathan, the fourteen-year-old tennis player, and
then review the character-building principles we
studied in this session:

- You build character by teaching your children the
  Scriptures.
- You build character by implementing a consistent
  system of discipline and rewards.
- You build character by continually training your
  children in the right way to live.
- You build character through your relationship
  with your children.

How would you apply these principles in Jonathan's
case?

Ultimately your goal is to point your children toward
a life of dependence upon God. If you teach them
God-honoring standards and then train them in how

to trust and obey God, they learn how to respond rightly to authority and to life's circumstances. As 3 John 4 says, "I have no greater joy than this, to hear of my children walking in the truth" (New American Standard Bible).

Make a Date

Make a date with your spouse to meet before the next session to complete this session's HomeBuilders Project.

DATE

TIME

LOCATION

HOMEBUILDERS PROJECT   60 MINUTES

As a Couple [10 minutes]

Review the list of personal characteristics on page 53.

- From the list or otherwise, what is a character quality your father or mother emphasized to you repeatedly while you were growing up? How well did they model this character quality to you?
- Which quality would you like to see better reflected in you? in your children?
- What is one characteristic you really appreciate in your spouse?

Individually [20 minutes]

Part One: Reflecting on Your Own Character

Since character is more "caught" than "taught," you can't expect your child to develop character qualities that you are not modeling yourself. The Scripture warns us that our sins (as parents) will be passed down through four generations unless we turn from them (Deuteronomy 5:9).

1. Evaluate yourself on the following character traits by putting a plus **(+)** by each trait that you think is a strength and a minus **(-)** by each trait you think is a current need.

___honest	___patient
___trustworthy	___joyous
___respectful	___faithful
___teachable	___self-controlled
___obedient	___courageous
___loving	___humble

___peaceful   ___hopeful

___gentle   ___giving

___kind   ___forgiving

___content   ___cooperative

2. What would you consider to be your two greatest character strengths and needs?

Part Two: Evaluating the Character Needs of Your Children

Use the following list to assess the character strengths and needs of your children. If you're going to evaluate more than one child, you may want to make copies of the list. (You have permission to copy the list on the next page for this purpose.)

You may not be able to complete this for each child; some may be too young to evaluate adequately.

3. Evaluate your child in the following areas by putting a plus **(+)** by each trait you would rate as a strength and a minus **(-)** mark by each trait you feel is a current need.

___honest	___patient
___trustworthy	___joyous
___respectful	___faithful
___teachable	___self-controlled
___obedient	___courageous
___loving	___humble
___peaceful	___hopeful
___gentle	___giving
___kind	___forgiving
___content	___cooperative

4. For each child you evaluated, what would you consider to be the two greatest character strengths and needs?

Interact as a Couple [30 minutes]

1. Discuss your answers from the individual section.

2. Start to develop a plan for continuing to build your children's character. Choose one or two needs for each child, and think through some action steps you can take to build the desired character traits in them. Keep in mind the process outlined in the group session:

- You build character by teaching your children the Scriptures.
- You build character by implementing a consistent system of discipline and rewards.
- You build character by continually training your children in the right way to live.
- You build character in your children through your relationship with your children.

3. Close in prayer. Ask God to help you model the character traits that you identified for your children.

Be sure to check out the related Parent-Child Interaction on page 100.

Training Your Children to Love Others

Children need to learn what it means to "love your neighbor as yourself."

WARM • UP   15   MINUTES

"Won't You Be My Neighbor?"

Choose one or two of the following questions to answer and share with the group:

- As a child, how well did you get along with your siblings? What did you tend to fight or argue about? How did your mom and dad deal with sibling rivalry?

- Thinking back to your childhood, who do you remember being your best neighbors? What makes them stand out?

- What's the nicest thing a neighbor has ever done for you?

(continued on next page)

- When you were growing up, who in your neighborhood or at school did you have trouble getting along with? Explain.

- When is a time you recall your family helping a stranger in need?

Project Report

Share one thing you learned from last session's HomeBuilders Project.

BLUEPRINTS   60 MINUTES

Children need parents who not only love them but also train them to love others. As a parent, you are God's number-one choice for teaching your children how to love others. As you develop a plan for building biblical character in your children, you will find that many character qualities focus on how they relate to other people.

The Second Greatest Commandment

1. Why is it important for parents to continually train their children to love others?

If you have a large group, form smaller groups of about six people to answer the Blueprints questions. Unless otherwise noted, answer the questions in your subgroup. Before moving into the Wrap-Up section, have subgroups report to the whole group the highlights from their discussion.

2. In Matthew 22:37, Jesus says that the greatest commandment is to "Love the Lord your God with all your heart and with all your soul and with all your mind." Then, in verse 39, he lists the second: "Love your neighbor as yourself." What do you think it means to love someone as yourself?

3. If children grow up not experiencing how to love others, what could be the impact on their relationships as adults?

HomeBuilders Principle:
Life, as God created it, revolves around relationships. Your influence plays a large role in your children's capacity to love others and to develop meaningful relationships.

What Does Love Look Like?

In Luke 10 Jesus shares the parable of the good Samaritan. This parable illustrates love in action and also answers the question "Who is my neighbor?"

4. Read Luke 10:25-37. According to this parable, what is the answer to the question "Who is my neighbor?" How can you help your children discover this truth?

5. Practically, what are some acts of mercy you can perform for your neighbors that could serve as an example to your children of "loving others as yourself"?

6. Romans 12:9-21 is one of many passages in Scripture that provides more specifics on how to love others. Read this passage, and then, in your group, list as many principles as you can find on how we should relate to other people.

7. Reviewing the principles that were just listed, which ones do your children need help with? Which ones do you need to work on? Write these down in your book.

Training Your Children

Parents training children to love others need to emphasize humility. Humility is not thinking less of oneself; it is thinking rightly about oneself in light of who God is. It is recognizing that God has all authority. It is remembering that we have disobeyed God and need the redemption that is possible only through his grace. And it is knowing that every person has great value because we all are made in God's image.

8. Read Philippians 2:1-4. What are several practical ways that humility affects relationships?

9. How can you practically help your child learn how to

- "do nothing out of selfish ambition"?

- "consider others better than yourselves"?

- "look not only to your own interests, but also to the interests of others"?

Another core issue for relationships is *respect for others.* One very practical way to show respect for others is by the words we use.

10. Read James 3:8-9. Think for a moment about your children and the words they use. How well do they use their words to show respect for others? What are some daily opportunities you have to train your children in this area?

11. How do humility and respect go hand in hand?

Because hurt and disappointment are a natural part of relationships, training your children to love others also means training them to *resolve conflict.*

Teaching your children to resolve conflict involves three key principles:

- *Listening:* Children need to learn to demonstrate respect by truly hearing what the other person is saying. As James 1:19 tells us, "My dear brothers, take note of this: Everyone should be quick to listen, slow to speak and slow to become angry."

- *Speaking the truth in love:* Children need to learn how to share their hurts in a way that does not threaten or accuse another person. Ephesians 4:15 says, "Instead, speaking the truth in love, we will in all things grow up into him who is the Head, that is, Christ."

- *Forgiving:* Children need to learn that forgiving means giving up the right to punish those who hurt or offend them. Ephesians 4:32: "Be kind and compassionate to one another, forgiving each other, just as in Christ God forgave you."

12. Think for a moment about each of your children and how they deal with conflict. In which of the three components— listening, speaking the truth in love, and forgiving—would you say your children are strongest? weakest? (Think of a corresponding example, if you can.)

Answer question 12 with your spouse. After answering, you may want to share an appropriate insight or discovery with the group.

As you raise your children, you'll find that training in resolving conflict is repetitive and tiresome. Remember, your children will behave and act like children. They need you to be the adult and train them to establish mature relationships.

W R A P • U P   15   M I N U T E S

Case Study

Your twelve-year-old son is shooting baskets outside with some friends, and his ten-year-old brother wants to play. Your older son reluctantly agrees but then joins the group in ridiculing his younger brother, who is not as athletically skilled. Your younger son becomes angry and throws the ball straight into the face of his older brother. This leads to a retaliatory elbow in the face, which leads to a chaotic scene of shouted accusations, tears, a bloody nose, and various bruises and scrapes.

As the parent on watch

- how would you handle this situation?
- how could this situation be used as a teachable moment about loving others?

Make a Date

Make a date with your spouse to meet before the next session to complete the HomeBuilders Project.

_____
DATE

_____
TIME

_____
LOCATION

HOMEBUILDERS PROJECT   6 0   M I N U T E S

As a Couple [10 minutes]

As an example of one way to love others, start this date by writing a short note of love and encouragement to each of your children.

Individually [20 minutes]

1. How has this session on training your children to love others challenged you as a parent?

2. Evaluate yourself in your relationships with others. For each of the following categories, circle the number you feel best applies to you.

Show respect for others	1	2	3	4	5	Show disrespect for others
Show love	1	2	3	4	5	Show animosity
Listen to others	1	2	3	4	5	Talk but don't listen
Speak the truth in love	1	2	3	4	5	Speak the truth without love
Forgive	1	2	3	4	5	Do not forgive
Regard the needs of others as more important	1	2	3	4	5	Want my own way
Praise others	1	2	3	4	5	Criticize others

3. Now rate your children in the same areas:

Child: _____

Shows respect for others	1	2	3	4	5	Shows disrespect for others
Shows love	1	2	3	4	5	Shows animosity
Listens to others	1	2	3	4	5	Talks but doesn't listen
Speaks the truth in love	1	2	3	4	5	Speaks the truth without love
Forgives	1	2	3	4	5	Does not forgive
Regards the needs of others as more important	1	2	3	4	5	Wants own way
Praises others	1	2	3	4	5	Criticizes others

Child: _____

Shows respect for others	1	2	3	4	5	Shows disrespect for others
Shows love	1	2	3	4	5	Shows animosity
Listens to others	1	2	3	4	5	Talks but doesn't listen

Speaks the truth in love	1	2	3	4	5	Speaks the truth without love
Forgives	1	2	3	4	5	Does not forgive
Regards the needs of others as more important	1	2	3	4	5	Wants own way
Praises others	1	2	3	4	5	Criticizes others

Child: _____

Shows respect for others	1	2	3	4	5	Shows disrespect for others
Shows love	1	2	3	4	5	Shows animosity
Listens to others	1	2	3	4	5	Talks but doesn't listen
Speaks the truth in love	1	2	3	4	5	Speaks the truth without love
Forgives	1	2	3	4	5	Does not forgive
Regards the needs of others as more important	1	2	3	4	5	Wants own way
Praises others	1	2	3	4	5	Criticizes others

4. Considering yourself as the model for your children, what would you say you have modeled well? What do you need to model better?

5. What is one relational quality that your spouse models well to your children?

Interact as a Couple [30 minutes]

1. Review your answers from the previous section.

2. Take a few minutes to analyze more specifically how your children love others. What are their strengths and weaknesses in the way they relate to

- friends?

- siblings?

- you?

- authority figures?

3. Discuss for each of your children what you think his or her biggest relationship needs are right now and in what areas he or she needs greater training.

4. Spend time in prayer, thanking God for your children and asking the Lord to give you the wisdom to train them to love others.

Be sure to check out the related Parent-Child Interaction on page 102.

Imparting a Sense of Purpose

As parents, we need to raise our children with the knowledge that they will be released to a life of mission and purpose.

W A R M • U P   15   M I N U T E S

Hopes and Expectations

Begin this session by brainstorming as a group a list of typical or common hopes and expectations that parents have for their children. After compiling a list, discuss these questions:

- From the list, what are one or two hopes or expectations your mom or dad had for you?

- What primary expectation or hope, from the list or otherwise, do you have for your children?

Project Report

Share one thing you learned from last session's HomeBuilders Project.

BLUEPRINTS   60 MINUTES

As parents, we have been given a great responsibility. We are called to teach and train our children about God and the Bible, to help lead them to a relationship with Christ, and to help them learn to walk with God.

All this is done with the knowledge that our children are moving toward adulthood. Although we will continue to play a key role in their lives, at some point we are responsible for letting our children go—"releasing" them as adults. For most of us, the major time of release comes when they move away from home, either to attend college or to live and work on their own.

Releasing Your Arrow

An appropriate metaphor for children is *arrows*. Psalm 127:3-4 tells us, "Behold, children are a gift of the Lord; The fruit of the womb is a reward. Like arrows in the hand of a warrior, So are the children of one's youth" (New American Standard Bible).

1. How is releasing a child into the world as an adult similar to releasing an arrow?

If you have a large group, form smaller groups of about six people to answer the Blueprints questions. Unless otherwise noted, answer the questions in your subgroup. Before moving into the Wrap-Up section, have subgroups report to the whole group the highlights from their discussion.

2. When did you leave home to be on your own? In what ways did you feel prepared? unprepared?

Before a child becomes an adult, there are actually a number of "release points." As children mature, there are some key stages when parents begin to let go of the control they've had and allow their children to make certain choices and assume certain responsibilities. For example, an early release point for young children is allowing them to play without constant direct supervision.

3. One key to preparing your children for a release point is to anticipate what outside influences your children will face and to build the type of character they need to face those influences.

Answer question 3 with your spouse. After answering, you may want to share an appropriate insight or discovery with the group.

- What is the next major "release point" you anticipate for each of your children?

- What influences will your children face at these points? (For example, anticipated influences for a child getting ready to start kindergarten could be things like peer pressure, exposure to bad language, added choices, and riding with strangers in a car or bus.)

- What can you be doing to prepare your children for their next anticipated release point?

HomeBuilders Principle:
God has designed your children to be released, not retained.

What Is Your Target?

The arrow described in Psalm 127:4 is an offensive weapon. It is launched toward a target, and it has an impact on whatever it hits. It is good for us as parents to determine exactly what our target is.

4. Why is it important to have a sense of purpose in life?

5. What do you think would be the most frequent replies if you talked with average Christian parents and asked, "When your children become adults, what should be their purpose in life?" What do you think their purpose in life should be?

6. What does Paul say in Philippians 1:21-26 about his purpose in life?

7. Read Matthew 28:18-20. How do you think this command of Jesus should be applied to your life? the lives of your children?

8. Now read Matthew 9:36-38.

- In what ways are people today "harassed and helpless, like sheep without a shepherd"?

- What do you think it means to be a worker in the harvest field?

HomeBuilders Principle:
Your children need to discover that there is no greater good than serving God by reaching out to people with the love of Christ.

Fulfilling Your Purpose

9. If you can, tell about a person you know who has a burning desire to reach out to others with the love of Christ. How is this mission practically lived out in the life of this person?

10. Why do you think many children in Christian families grow up without a strong conviction that they are to have an impact on their world for Christ?

11. What are practical ways we as parents can help develop a sense of purpose in our children?

12. Your children can be encouraged to have an impact on others. What are some ways your children could reach out to others right now? during the next year or two?

W R A P • U P   15 M I N U T E S

Parting Thoughts

As you come to the end of this course, take a few minutes to reflect on this experience. Review the following questions, and write down responses to the questions you can answer. Then relate to the group one or more of your answers.

- What has this group meant to you over the course of this study? Be specific.

- What is the most valuable thing that you have learned or discovered?

- How have you as a parent been changed or challenged?

- What would you like to see happen next for this group?

Make a Date

Make a date with your spouse to meet in the next week to complete the last HomeBuilders Project of this study.

DATE

TIME

LOCATION

As a Couple [10 minutes]

Take a look at the parenting mission statement you drafted during Wrap-Up in Session One (p. 19). Discuss how you see your mission now. Is it the same, or has it changed? Is there anything you want to change in or add to your mission statement?

Individually [20 minutes]

1. Overall, what has been the most important insight or lesson for you from this course?

2. Thinking about this course, what is at least one point of action you identified during this course that you want to implement to become a more effective parent?

3. What expectations did you have going into this study? How did your experience compare to your expectations?

4. As we discussed in the group session, releasing your children demands that you must have a target. What are your top goals for your children?

5. In what ways have these goals changed since you began this study?

Releasing your children involves several steps:

- anticipating outside influences,
- building God-honoring character to prepare your children to make good choices,
- maintaining accountability when appropriate, and
- trusting God.

6. What are one or two major outside influences you anticipate each of your children is likely to face

- in the short-term (within the next six months)?

- in the next one to two years?

7. With regard to the anticipated influences you identified for your children, think through these questions:

- What character qualities will help your children make good choices in these situations?
- What specific choices can you help your children decide in advance?
- What questions can you ask before and after these situations to help determine how your children behaved?

- How can you entrust your children to God in these situations?
- What fears do you have that need to be given over to God?

Interact as a Couple [30 minutes]

1. Review and discuss your responses to the previous questions.

2. For each child, choose a primary point of application from this course that you want to implement during the next month.

3. Evaluate things you can do to strengthen your home. You may want to consider continuing the practice of regularly setting aside time for date nights. You may also want to look at the list of ideas on page 111.

4. Close by reading Colossians 1:9-14, and then pray, adapting Paul's prayer into a prayer for your children.

Be sure to check out the related Parent-Child Interaction on page 104.

Please visit our Web site at www.familylife.com/homebuilders to give us your feedback on this study and to get information on other FamilyLife resources and conferences.

Parent-Child
Interactions

Contents

Parent-Child Interaction 1:..94

It's Puzzling

Parent-Child Interaction 2:..96

Sharing Your Faith Story

Parent-Child Interaction 3:..98

Family Prayer Journal

Parent-Child Interaction 4:..100

Profiles in Courage

Parent-Child Interaction 5:..102

Loving Your Neighbor

Parent-Child Interaction 6:..104

What's Your Target?

It's Puzzling

The following exercise was a big hit for many years with our sixth-grade Sunday school class. It will help your children recognize the futility of going through life without a plan for how it should be lived. That plan comes from God's Word.

For this exercise you will need a jigsaw puzzle, preferably one with about one hundred pieces that your children can put together. Make sure the box top or another picture of the completed puzzle is available. You might want to buy a new puzzle they haven't seen before.

If you have at least two children who are able to complete puzzles on their own, a variation of this exercise would be to use two similar puzzles and make it a contest.

1. Dump the pieces from the puzzle onto a table, but don't show your children the completed picture. (If the picture is on the box top, we suggest hiding it.) Tell the children they have about ten minutes to get as much of the puzzle finished as possible. If they ask about the box top, tell them it's not available. Be sure to let them go at least eight minutes. The point is to let them experience the frustration of trying to complete a puzzle when they can't see what it should look like.

2. After ten minutes, bring out the picture and say, "Now let's see what changes when you can see this." Let them work on the puzzle for another five minutes.

3. Then ask the following questions:

- "What did you learn from this exercise?"
- "How did it feel to try to complete the puzzle without the box top?"

4. Have one of your children read Psalm 19:7-11. Ask, "What do we learn about the benefits of knowing and obeying God's Word?"

5. Then ask, "How would you compare having God's Word to guide us to having the picture to guide you when you were doing the puzzle?"

Sharing Your Faith Story

Children need to see a real, dynamic, living, obedient faith in Christ in their parents. It will help them see their need for a personal relationship with Christ, and it will provide a model of how to walk in faith. This special family time gives you and your spouse the opportunity to tell your children about your spiritual journey.

Before you meet with your children, spend some time putting together your personal faith story. Follow the model of Paul in Acts 26:1-23:

- Start by briefly recapping what your life was like before you met Christ.

- Talk about how God brought you to an awareness of your need for him and your faith commitment experience—how you came into a personal relationship with Christ.

- Then tell about the changes God has made in your life, what your life has been like since making a personal commitment to follow Christ. You may also want to mention the people (parents, relatives, pastors, Sunday school teachers, schoolteachers, or others) God has used in your life to help you grow in your faith.

1. Have one of your children read Psalm 78:1-8. Ask, "What does this passage talk about parents doing with their children?"

2. Tell your family that one way you can follow the words of Psalm 78 is to tell them about some of the things God has done in your life. Then share your faith story.

3. If some of your children have already made a personal commitment to Christ, let them tell about their experience also. If they have trouble remembering details of the past, help them by sharing what you remember about when they confessed their need for Christ.

Going through this exercise with your children may give you insight into their spiritual condition. Don't assume your children are Christians just because they were baptized or because they once verbalized a prayer to receive Christ. Some children say the right words but don't understand what it means to be a Christian. We suggest consulting the evangelistic resources listed on our "Recommended Resources" list on pages 150-151.

Family Prayer Journal

One of the most important ways to teach a child about the living God is to help them become personally aware that God exists and answers our prayers. Answered prayer is a powerful testimony of God's existence.

1. Begin by telling about times that God answered specific prayer requests for you in the past.

2. Have your children look up Philippians 4:6-7, James 4:2-3, and 1 John 5:14-15. Ask, "What do we learn about prayer from these passages?"

Make it clear that God promises to meet our needs, but not all our desires. Sometimes our desires are self-centered. Also remind everyone that God answers our prayers in different ways. God may say yes and simply fulfill a need or desire. God may also say no or not respond for some length of time or respond in an unexpected way. Since God's will is perfect, God may withhold responses to our prayers because God knows the best time to answer our prayers.

3. Start a family prayer notebook. To make it special, you may want to let your children help prepare it and decorate it.

4. This step is essential to building your children's faith: In your family prayer notebook, write your family's prayer requests. Do this now, and add family prayer requests on a regular basis. As God answers your family's prayers, take out your prayer notebook and record how and when God answered the prayer. Praise God for his provision, and talk to your children about the times an answer is delayed or is different from what was asked for. It is important to thank God for his sovereign control in our lives, even when we experience disappointment in how we thought or wanted God to work.

Your prayer notebook will become a living journal of God's direct intervention in your lives. Periodically reviewing what God has done in your family will affirm God's existence and strengthen each person's faith.

Profiles in Courage

As you build character in your children, take advantage of the many stories in the Bible about people who displayed God-honoring character qualities. One of the best is the story of three friends of Daniel—Shadrach, Meshach, and Abednego—who courageously decided to obey God and refused to worship King Nebuchadnezzar.

Before you meet, think of some practical ways each of your children could display courage in obeying God no matter what the consequences. A young child, for example, could obey God by refusing to lie about doing something wrong even though it may mean getting punished. A teenager could courageously obey God by honoring and obeying his or her parents— even when friends may try to persuade him or her to do otherwise.

1. Ask, "What do you think courage is? What does it mean to be courageous?" If you can, share with your children the most courageous thing you've ever done.

2. Say, "One way of describing courage is that it's having the strength to do the right thing even when it's difficult or dangerous." Then have the family turn to Daniel 3 and instruct someone to read aloud the first eleven verses. Ask, "What do you think was so wrong about what the king wanted the people to do?" (You may also want to have someone read Exodus 20:1-6.)

3. Instruct someone to read Daniel 3:12-18, then ask, "What is courageous about what Shadrach, Meshach, and Abednego did?"

4. Have someone read Daniel 3:19-30. Then ask two questions, "Do you think Shadrach, Meshach, and Abednego knew ahead of time that God would spare their lives?" and "How did God bless them for their obedience and for doing the right thing?"

5. Finally ask, "What are some ways we can be courageous? What are some situations we face that call for us to obey God, no matter what happens?" Take this opportunity to praise your children for courageous choices they have made in the past.

6. *(Optional)* Think of choices your children will probably face in the next year or two that will require courage. Describe one of these situations, and then ask your children what they would do. For example: "What would you do if a friend offers you a ride home in his or her car, and when you get in you discover this person has been drinking?"

Interaction 5

Loving Your Neighbor

Your children can benefit from a practical opportunity to put into practice the words of Matthew 22:37-39. When asked what the greatest commandment was, Jesus replied, " 'Love the Lord your God with all your heart and with all your soul and with all your mind.' This is the first and greatest commandment. And the second is like it: 'Love your neighbor as yourself.' "

In your community and church, many elderly people need help. Ask the Lord to lead you to a widow or elderly couple your family could help on a regular basis. You might want to consider adopting the widow or couple as "adopted grandparent(s)." If you aren't sure where you can find someone who has ongoing needs, contact your church or an agency in your community that works with seniors.

Here are some of things you might do as a family for your adopted grandparents:

- Take care of their yard for a summer.
- Clean the rain gutters on their house.
- Help clean up their house, garage, or attic.
- Take them out shopping.
- Cook fresh goodies.
- Organize special photos into a memory book.

Make it a goal to serve these people and expect nothing in return. What you will most likely see happen is that, as you serve others, God will give you a love for them. It is difficult to serve someone and not experience a God-inspired love for the person that you did not have before.

What's Your Target?

This is the last project you will do during this HomeBuilders study. It may also be the most important, because it will give you the opportunity to show your children your goals for their lives and to call them to the highest cause of all—following Christ and taking God's Word to their world.

To prepare for this time, you will need to complete the HomeBuilders Project that starts on page 89 with your spouse. Question 4 in the section in which you work individually calls for you to write down your top goals for your children. Transfer these goals to the target diagram that follows. We assume that your top goal will be for your children to know and walk with God, so be sure to put that in the space for the bull's-eye.

1. Read Psalm 127:3-5a: "Behold, children are a gift of the Lord, the fruit of the womb is a reward. Like arrows in the hand of a warrior, so are the children of one's youth. How blessed is the man whose quiver is full of them" (NASB).

2. Ask, "Why do you think the Bible tells us that children are a gift from God?"

YOUR GOALS FOR YOUR CHILDREN

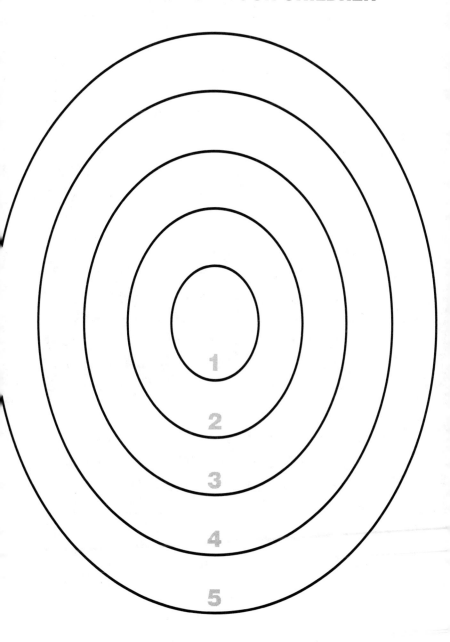

After your children answer, take a few moments to tell them some of the ways they have been a blessing for you.

3. Ask, "What are we supposed to do with arrows? What are they made for?"

If you have older children, you may want to incorporate a family outing to an archery range as a part of this exercise to see the arrow illustration in action. With younger children, consider using a safe toy bow-and-arrow set to demonstrate the arrow illustration.

4. Say, "The verses we read told us that children are 'like arrows in the hand of a warrior.' How do you think children are like arrows?"

5. Say, "Eventually, all arrows need to be released. And so it is with children—eventually, we will release you, and you will live on your own. One thing that's important for us as parents is to release you in the right direction, to the right target."

6. Ask, "What do you think are some good goals for your lives?" After your children name their goals, show them the target in which you've written goals for their lives.

7. Ask, "Why do you think we've put your relationship with God at the center of the target?"

8. Have your children read Matthew 9:35-38, Matthew 22:36-39, and Matthew 28:18-20. After each passage is read, ask, "What do you think God is trying to tell us through this passage?" Use this opportunity to tell your children that the most important thing for them to do with their lives is to serve God and reach out to people with the love of Christ.

Where Do You Go From Here?

It is our prayer that you have benefited greatly from this study in the HomeBuilders Parenting Series. We hope that your marriage and home will continue to grow stronger as you both submit your lives to Jesus Christ and build according to his blueprints.

We also hope that you will begin reaching out to strengthen other marriages in your community and local church. Your church needs couples like you who are committed to building Christian marriages. A favorite World War II story illustrates this point very clearly.

The year was 1940. The French Army had just collapsed under Hitler's onslaught. The Dutch had folded, overwhelmed by the Nazi regime. The Belgians had surrendered. And the British Army was trapped on the coast of France in the channel port of Dunkirk.

Two hundred and twenty thousand of Britain's finest young men seemed doomed to die, turning the English Channel red with their blood. The Fuehrer's troops, only miles away in the hills of France, didn't realize how close to victory they actually were.

Any rescue seemed feeble and futile in the time remaining. A "thin" British Navy—"the professionals"—told King George VI that at best they could save 17,000 troops. The House of Commons was warned to prepare for "hard and heavy tidings."

Politicians were paralyzed. The king was powerless. And the Allies could only watch as spectators from a distance. Then as the doom of the British Army seemed imminent, a strange fleet appeared on the horizon of the English Channel—the wildest assortment of boats perhaps ever assembled in history.

Trawlers, tugs, scows, fishing sloops, lifeboats, pleasure craft, smacks and coasters, sailboats, even the London fire-brigade flotilla. *Each ship was manned by civilian volunteers—English fathers sailing to rescue Britain's exhausted, bleeding sons.*

William Manchester writes in his epic book, *The Last Lion*, that even today what happened in 1940 in less than twenty-four hours seems like a miracle—not only were all of the British soldiers rescued, but 118,000 other Allied troops as well.

Today the Christian home is much like those troops at Dunkirk. Pressured, trapped, and demoralized, it needs help. Your help. The Christian community may be much like England—we stand waiting for politicians, professionals, even for our pastors to step in and save the family. But the problem is much larger than all of those combined can solve.

With the highest divorce rate of any nation on earth, we need an all-out effort by men and women who are determined to help rescue the exhausted and wounded casualties of today's families. We need an outreach effort by common couples with faith in an uncommon God.

May we challenge you to invest your lives in others? You have one of the greatest opportunities in history—to help save today's families. By starting a HomeBuilders group, you can join couples around the world who are building and rebuilding hundreds of thousands of homes with a new, solid foundation of a relationship with God.

Will You Join Us in "Touching Lives...Changing Families"?

The following are some practical ways you can make a difference in families today:

1. Gather a group of four to eight couples, and lead them through the six sessions of this HomeBuilders study, *Raising Children of Faith.* (Why not consider challenging others in your church or community to form additional HomeBuilders groups?)

2. Commit to continue building your marriage and home by doing another course in the HomeBuilders Parenting Series or by leading a study in the HomeBuilders Couples Series.

3. An excellent outreach tool is the film *JESUS,* which is available on video. For more information, contact FamilyLife at 1-800-FL-TODAY.

4. Host a dinner party. Invite families from your neighborhood to your home, and as a couple share your faith in Christ.

5. Reach out and share the love of Christ with neighborhood children.

6. If you have attended the Weekend to Remember conference, why not offer to assist your pastor in counseling couples engaged to be married, using the material you received?

For more information about any of the above ministry opportunities, contact your local church, or write:

> **FamilyLife**
> P.O. Box 8220
> Little Rock, AR 72221-8220
> 1-800-FL-TODAY
> **www.familylife.com**

Our Problems, God's Answers

Every couple eventually has to deal with problems in marriage. Communication problems. Parenting issues. Money problems. Difficulties with sexual intimacy. These issues are important to cultivating a strong, loving relationship with your spouse. HomeBuilders Bible studies are designed to help you strengthen your marriage and family in many of these critical areas.

Part One: The Big Problem

One basic problem is at the heart of every other problem in every marriage, and it's a problem we can't help you fix. No matter how hard you try, this is one problem that is too big for you to deal with on your own.

The problem is separation from God. If you want to experience marriage the way it was designed to be, you need a vital relationship with the God who created you and offers you the power to live a life of joy and purpose.

And what separates us from God is one more problem—sin. Most of us have assumed throughout our lives that the term "sin" refers to a list of bad habits that everyone agrees are wrong. We try to deal with our sin problem by working hard to become better people. We read books to learn how to control our anger, or we resolve to stop cheating on our taxes.

But in our hearts, we know our sin problem runs much deeper than a list of bad habits. All of us have rebelled against God. We have ignored him and have decided to run our own lives in a way that makes sense to us. The Bible says that the God who created us wants us to follow his plan for our lives. But because of our sin problem, we think our ideas and plans are better than his.

- *"For all have sinned and fall short of the glory of God"* (Romans 3:23).

What does it mean to "fall short of the glory of God"? It means that none of us has trusted and treasured God the way we should. We have sought to satisfy ourselves with other things and have treated those things as more valuable than God. We have gone our own way. According to the Bible, we have to pay a penalty for our sin. We cannot simply do things the way we choose and hope it will all be OK with God. Following our own plan leads to our destruction.

- *"There is a way that seems right to a man, but in the end it leads to death"* (Proverbs 14:12).

- *"For the wages of sin is death"* (Romans 6:23a).

The penalty for sin is that we are forever separated from God's love. God is holy, and we are sinful. No matter how hard we try, we cannot come up with some plan, like living a good life or even trying to do what the Bible says, and hope that we can avoid the penalty.

God's Solution to Sin

Thankfully, God has a way to solve our dilemma. He became a man through the person of Jesus Christ. He lived a holy life, in perfect obedience to God's plan. He also willingly died on a cross to pay our penalty for sin. Then he proved that he is more powerful than sin or death by rising from the dead. He alone has the power to overrule the penalty for our sin.

- *"Jesus answered, 'I am the way and the truth and the life. No one comes to the Father except through me' "* (John 14:6).

- *"But God demonstrates his own love for us in this: While we were still sinners, Christ died for us"* (Romans 5:8).

- *"Christ died for our sins...he was buried...he was raised on the third day according to the Scriptures...he appeared to Peter, and then to the Twelve. After that, he appeared to more than five hundred"* (1 Corinthians 15:3-6).

- *"For the wages of sin is death, but the gift of God is eternal life in Christ Jesus our Lord"* (Romans 6:23).

The death of Jesus has fixed our sin problem. He has bridged the gap between God and us. He is calling all of us to come to him and to give up our own flawed plan for how to run our lives. He wants us to trust God and his plan.

Accepting God's Solution

If you agree that you are separated from God, he is calling you to confess your sins. All of us have made messes of our lives because we have stubbornly preferred our ideas and plans over his. As a result, we deserve to be cut off from God's love and his care for us. But God has promised that if we will agree that we have rebelled against his plan for us and have messed up our lives, he will forgive us and will fix our sin problem.

- *"Yet to all who received him, to those who believed in his name, he gave the right to become children of God"* (John 1:12).

- *"For it is by grace you have been saved, through faith—and this not from yourselves, it is the gift of*

God—not by works, so that no one can boast" (Ephesians 2:8-9).

When the Bible talks about receiving Christ, it means we acknowledge that we are sinners and that we can't fix the problem ourselves. It means we turn away from our sin. And it means we trust Christ to forgive our sins and to make us the kind of people he wants us to be. It's not enough to just intellectually believe that Christ is the Son of God. We must trust in him and his plan for our lives by faith, as an act of the will.

Are things right between you and God, with him and his plan at the center of your life? Or is life spinning out of control as you seek to make your way on your own?

You can decide today to make a change. You can turn to Christ and allow him to transform your life. All you need to do is to talk to him and tell him what is stirring in your mind and in your heart. If you've never done this before, consider taking the steps listed here:

- Do you agree that you need God? Tell God.

- Have you made a mess of your life by following your own plan? Tell God.

- Do you want God to forgive you? Tell God.

- Do you believe that Jesus' death on the cross and his resurrection from the dead gave him the power to fix your sin problem and to grant you the gift of eternal life? Tell God.

- Are you ready to acknowledge that God's plan for your life is better than any plan you could come up with? Tell God.

- Do you agree that God has the right to be the Lord and master of your life? Tell God.

"Seek the Lord while he may be found;
call on him while he is near"
(Isaiah 55:6).

Following is a suggested prayer:

Lord Jesus, I need you. Thank you for dying on the
cross for my sins. I receive you as my Savior and Lord.
Thank you for forgiving my sins and giving me eternal
life. Make me the kind of person you want me to be.

Does this prayer express the desire of your heart? If it
does, pray it right now, and Christ will come into your life, as
he promised.

Part Two: Living the Christian Life

For a person who is a follower of Christ—a Christian—the
penalty for sin is paid in full. But the effect of sin continues
throughout our lives.

- *"If we claim to be without sin, we deceive ourselves*
  and the truth is not in us" (1 John 1:8).

- *"For what I do is not the good I want to do; no,*
  the evil I do not want to do—this I keep on doing"
  (Romans 7:19).

The effects of sin carry over into our marriages as well.
Even Christians struggle to maintain solid, God-honoring marriages. Most couples eventually realize that they can't do it on
their own. But with God's help, they can succeed. The Holy
Spirit can have a huge impact in the marriages of Christians
who live constantly, moment by moment, under his gracious
direction.

Self-Centered Christians

Many Christians struggle to live the Christian life in their own strength because they are not allowing God to control their lives. Their interests are self-directed, often resulting in failure and frustration.

- *"Brothers, I could not address you as spiritual but as worldly—mere infants in Christ. I gave you milk, not solid food, for you were not yet ready for it. Indeed, you are still not ready. You are still worldly. For since there is jealousy and quarreling among you, are you not worldly? Are you not acting like mere men?"* (1 Corinthians 3:1-3).

The self-centered Christian cannot experience the abundant and fruitful Christian life. Such people trust in their own efforts to live the Christian life: They are either uninformed about—or have forgotten—God's love, forgiveness, and power. This kind of Christian

- has an up-and-down spiritual experience.

- cannot understand himself—he wants to do what is right, but cannot.

- fails to draw upon the power of the Holy Spirit to live the Christian life.

Some or all of the following traits may characterize the Christian who does not fully trust God:

disobedience	plagued by impure thoughts
lack of love for God and others	jealous
	worrisome
inconsistent prayer life	easily discouraged, frustrated
lack of desire for Bible study	critical
legalistic attitude	lack of purpose

Note: The individual who professes to be a Christian but who continues to practice sin should realize that he may not be a Christian at all, according to Ephesians 5:5 and 1 John 2:3; 3:6, 9.

Spirit-Centered Christians

When a Christian puts Christ on the throne of his life, he yields to God's control. This Christian's interests are directed by the Holy Spirit, resulting in harmony with God's plan.

- *"But the fruit of the Spirit is love, joy, peace, patience, kindness, goodness, faithfulness, gentleness and self-control. Against such things there is no law"* (Galatians 5:22-23).

Jesus said:

- *"I have come that they may have life, and have it to the full"* (John 10:10b).

- *"I am the vine; you are the branches. If a man remains in me and I in him, he will bear much fruit; apart from me you can do nothing"* (John 15:5).

- *"But you will receive power when the Holy Spirit comes on you; and you will be my witnesses in Jerusalem, and in all Judea and Samaria, and to the ends of the earth"* (Acts 1:8).

The following traits result naturally from the Holy Spirit's work in our lives:

Christ centered	love
Holy Spirit empowered	joy
motivated to tell others about Jesus	peace
	patience
dedicated to prayer	kindness
student of God's Word	goodness
trusts God	faithfulness
obeys God	gentleness
	self-control

The degree to which these traits appear in a Christian's life and marriage depends upon the extent to which the Christian trusts the Lord with every detail of life, and upon that person's maturity in Christ. One who is only beginning to understand the ministry of the Holy Spirit should not be discouraged if he is not as fruitful as mature Christians who have known and experienced this truth for a longer period of time.

Giving God Control

Jesus promises his followers an abundant and fruitful life as they allow themselves to be directed and empowered by the Holy Spirit. As we give God control of our lives, Christ lives in and through us in the power of the Holy Spirit (John 15).

If you sincerely desire to be directed and empowered by God, you can turn your life over to the control of the Holy Spirit right now (Matthew 5:6; John 7:37-39).

First, confess your sins to God, agreeing with him that you want to turn from any past sinful patterns in your life. Thank God in faith that he has forgiven all of your sins because Christ died for you (Colossians 2:13-15; 1 John 1:9; 2:1-3; Hebrews 10:1-18).

Be sure to offer every area of your life to God (Romans 12:1-2). Consider what areas you might rather keep to yourself, and be sure you're willing to give God control in those areas.

By faith, commit yourself to living according to the Holy Spirit's guidance and power.

- *Live by the Spirit:* **"So I say, live by the Spirit, and you will not gratify the desires of the sinful nature. For the sinful nature desires what is contrary to the Spirit, and the Spirit what is contrary to the sinful nature. They are in conflict with each other, so that you do not do what you want"** (Galatians 5:16-17).

- *Trust in God's promise:* **"This is the confidence we have in approaching God: that if we ask anything according to his will, he hears us. And if we know that he hears us—whatever we ask—we know that we have what we asked of him"** (1 John 5:14-15).

Expressing Your Faith Through Prayer

Prayer is one way of expressing your faith to God. If the prayer that follows expresses your sincere desire, consider praying the prayer or putting the thoughts into your own words:

> **Dear God, I need you. I acknowledge that I have been directing my own life and that, as a result, I have sinned against you. I thank you that you have forgiven my sins through Christ's death on the cross for me. I now invite Christ to take his place on the throne of my life. Take control of my life through the Holy Spirit as you promised you would if I asked in faith. I now thank you for directing my life and for empowering me through the Holy Spirit.**

Walking in the Spirit

If you become aware of an area of your life (an attitude or an action) that is displeasing to God, simply confess your sin, and thank God that he has forgiven your sins on the basis of Christ's death on the cross. Accept God's love and forgiveness by faith, and continue to have fellowship with him.

If you find that you've taken back control of your life through sin—a definite act of disobedience—try this exercise, "Spiritual Breathing," as you give that control back to God.

1. Exhale. Confess your sin. Agree with God that you've sinned against him, and thank him for his forgiveness of it, according to 1 John 1:9 and Hebrews 10:1-25. Remember that confession involves repentance, a determination to change attitudes and actions.

2. Inhale. Surrender control of your life to Christ, inviting the Holy Spirit to once again take charge. Trust that he now directs and empowers you, according to the command of Galatians 5:16-17 and the promise of 1 John 5:14-15. Returning to your faith in God enables you to continue to experience God's love and forgiveness.

Revolutionizing Your Marriage

This new commitment of your life to God will enrich your marriage. Sharing with your spouse what you've committed to is a powerful step in solidifying this commitment. As you exhibit the Holy Spirit's work within you, your spouse may be drawn to make the same commitment you've made. If both of you have given control of your lives to the Holy Spirit, you'll be able to help each other remain true to God, and your marriage may be revolutionized. With God in charge of your lives, life becomes an amazing adventure.

Leaders Notes

Contents

About Leading a HomeBuilders Group **124**

About the Leaders Notes **128**

Session One **129**

Session Two **134**

Session Three **138**

Session Four **142**

Session Five **145**

Session Six **147**

About Leading a HomeBuilders Group

What is the leader's job?

Your role is that of "facilitator"—one who encourages people to think and to discover what Scripture says, who helps group members feel comfortable, and who keeps things moving forward.

What is the best setting and time schedule for this study?

This study is designed as a small-group home Bible study. However, it can be adapted for use in a Sunday school setting as well. Here are some suggestions for using this study in a small group and in a Sunday school class:

In a small group

To create a friendly and comfortable atmosphere, it is recommended that you do this study in a home setting. In many cases, the couple that leads the study also serves as host to the group. Sometimes involving another couple as host is a good idea. Choose the option you believe will work best for your group, taking into account factors such as the number of couples participating and the location.

Each session is designed as a ninety-minute study, but we recommend a two-hour block of time. This will allow you to move through each part of the study at a more relaxed pace. However, be sure to keep in mind one of the cardinal rules of a small group: Good groups start *and* end on time. People's time is valuable, and your group will appreciate your being respectful of this.

In a Sunday school class

There are two important adaptations you need to make if you want to use this study in a class setting: (1) The material you cover should focus on the content from the Blueprints section of each session. Blueprints is the heart of each session and is designed to last sixty minutes. (2) Most Sunday school classes are taught in a teacher format instead of a small-group format. If this study will be used in a class setting, the class should adapt to a small-group dynamic. This will involve an interactive, discussion-based format and may also require a class to break into multiple smaller groups (we recommend groups of six to eight people).

What is the best size group?

We recommend from four to eight couples (including you and your spouse). If you have more people interested than you think you can accommodate, consider asking someone else to lead a second group. If you have a large group, you are encouraged at various times in the study to break into smaller subgroups. This helps you cover the material in a timely fashion and allows for optimum interaction and participation within the group.

What about refreshments?

Many groups choose to serve refreshments, which help create an environment of fellowship. If you plan on including refreshments in your study, here are a couple of suggestions: (1) For the first session (or two) you should provide the refreshments and then allow the group to be involved by having people sign up to bring them on later dates. (2) Consider starting your group with a short time of informal fellowship and refreshments (fifteen minutes), then move into the study. If couples are late, they miss only the food and don't disrupt the study. You may also want to have refreshments available at the end of your meeting to encourage fellowship, but remember, respect the group members' time by ending the study on schedule and allowing anyone who needs to leave right away the opportunity to do so gracefully.

What about child care?

Groups handle this differently depending on their needs. Here are a couple of options you may want to consider:

- Have group members be responsible for making their own arrangements.
- As a group, hire child care, and have all the kids watched in one location.

What about prayer?

An important part of a small group is prayer. However, as the leader, you need to be sensitive to the level of comfort the people in your group have toward praying in front of others. Never call on people to pray aloud if you don't know if they are comfortable doing this. There are a number of creative approaches you can take, such as modeling prayer, calling for volunteers, and letting people state their prayers in the form of finishing a sentence. A tool that is helpful in a group is a prayer list. You are encouraged to utilize a prayer list, but let it be someone else's ministry to the group. You should lead the prayer time, but allow another couple in the group the opportunity to create, update, and distribute prayer lists.

In closing

An excellent resource that covers leading a HomeBuilders group in greater detail is the *HomeBuilders Leader Guide* by Drew and Kit Coons. This book may be obtained at your local Christian bookstore or by contacting Group Publishing or FamilyLife.

About the Leaders Notes

The sessions in this study can be easily led without a lot of preparation time. However, accompanying Leaders Notes have been provided to assist you in preparation. The categories within the Leaders Notes are as follows:

Objectives

The purpose of the Objectives is to help you focus on the issues that will be presented in each session.

Notes and Tips

This section will relate any general comments about the session. This information should be viewed as ideas, helps, and suggestions. You may want to create a checklist of things you want to be sure to do in each session.

Commentary

Included in this section are notes that relate specifically to Blueprints questions. Not all Blueprints questions in each session will have accompanying commentary notes. Questions with related commentaries are designated by numbers (for example, Blueprints question 5 in Session One would correspond to number 5 in the Commentary section of Session One Leaders Notes).

Session One:
Your Job as a Parent

Objectives

We need to look to God and the Bible to discover the values we need to pass on to our children.

In this session, parents will...

- enjoy getting to know one another.

- identify the challenges of being a parent today.

- reflect on the goals and dreams they have for their children.

- examine what the Bible says about their responsibilities as parents.

Notes and Tips

1. Welcome to the first session of the HomeBuilders course *Raising Children of Faith*. While it is anticipated that most of the participants in this HomeBuilders Parenting Series study will be couples with children, be aware that you may have single parents, future parents, or even one parent from a marriage participating. Welcome everyone warmly, and work to create a supportive and encouraging environment.

You will find that certain features throughout this study are specifically geared toward couples, such as designated couples' questions and the HomeBuilders Projects. However, we encourage you as the leader to be flexible and sensitive to your group. For example, if you have a single parent in your group, you might invite that person to join you and your spouse when a couples' question is indicated in the study. Or if there are multiple single parents, you may want to encourage them to join together for these questions. Likewise, for the HomeBuilders Projects at the end of every session, you may want to encourage singles to complete what they can individually or to work with another single parent on the project.

2. If you have not already done so, you will want to read the "About the Sessions" information on pages 4 and 5, as well as "About Leading a HomeBuilders Group" and "About the Leaders Notes" starting on page 124.

3. As part of the first session, you may want to review with the group some ground rules (see page 11 in the Introduction).

4. Be sure you have a study guide for each person. You will also want to have extra Bibles and pens or pencils.

5. Depending on the size of your group, you may spend longer than fifteen minutes on the Warm-Up section. If this happens, try to finish the Blueprints section in forty-five to sixty minutes. It is a good idea to mark the questions in Blueprints that you want to be sure to cover. Encourage couples to look at any questions you don't get to during the session when they do the HomeBuilders Project for this session.

6. You will notice a note in the margin at the start of the Blueprints section that recommends breaking into smaller

groups. The reason for this is twofold: (1) to help facilitate discussion and participation by everyone, and (2) to help you be able to get through the material in the allotted time.

7. Throughout the sessions in this course, you will find questions that are designed for spouses to answer together (like question 7 in this session). The purpose of these "couples' questions" is to foster communication and unity between spouses and to give couples an opportunity to deal with personal issues. While couples are free to share their responses to these questions with the group, respect that not all couples will want to do so.

8. With this group just getting under way, it's not too late to invite another couple to join the group. During Wrap-Up, challenge everyone to think about a couple to invite to the next session.

9. Before dismissing, make a special point to tell the group about the importance of the HomeBuilders Project. Encourage each couple to "Make a Date" before the next meeting to complete the project. Mention that there will be an opportunity during the next session to report on their experiences with the project.

10. To conclude this first session, you may want to offer a closing prayer instead of asking others to pray aloud. Many people are uncomfortable praying in front of others, and unless you already know your group well, it may be wise to slowly venture into various methods of prayer.

Commentary

Here is some additional information about various Blueprints questions. The numbers that follow correspond to the Blueprints questions of the same numbers in the session. Be aware that notes are not included for every question. Many of the questions in this study are designed so that group members will draw from their own opinions and experiences. If you share any of these points, be sure to do so in a manner that does not stifle discussion by making you the authority with *the real answers*. Begin your comments by saying things like, "One thing I notice in this passage is…" or "I think another reason for this is…"

5. On one hand, parents want the best for their children and want them to have fun participating in various activities. But many also believe that the success of their children rests largely on their ability to perform well in school and to develop a variety of skills.

6. Many children today are so busy that they do not have adequate time to play, rest, and just be with their families. Also, parents can become so preoccupied with extracurricular activities that they do not spend enough time developing God-honoring character in their children.

8. These two passages speak about the primary responsibilities of parents. More than anything else, we are responsible for telling our children about God, what God has done, and what God has commanded. We are to talk about God and his Word throughout the day, as a way of life.

The values we are to pass on to our children also focus on God. We are to teach children to trust God, to not forget

God's deeds, to keep God's commandments, and to love God with all their heart and soul and strength.

Attention HomeBuilders Leaders

FamilyLife invites you to register your HomeBuilders group. Your registration connects you to the HomeBuilders Leadership Network, a worldwide movement of couples who are using HomeBuilders to strengthen marriages and families in their communities. You'll receive the latest news about HomeBuilders and other ministry opportunities to help strengthen marriages and families in your community. As the HomeBuilders Leadership Network grows, we will offer additional resources such as online training, prayer requests, and chat with authors. There is no cost or obligation to register; simply go to www.familylife.com/homebuilders.

Session Two:
Introducing Your Children to God

Objectives

Children need to understand the basics of who God is and how to establish a relationship with him.

In this session parents will...

• reflect on their own spiritual upbringing.

• recognize their need to assume responsibility for teaching their children about God.

• work through some basic questions about God in order to be able to help their children discover how to have a personal relationship with God.

Notes and Tips

1. With the subject of a personal relationship with God being addressed, this is an excellent session to assess where individuals are spiritually. Make a point to follow up with those who are spiritually open but who may have questions. You may want to suggest to the group, for further reading, the article "Our Problems, God's Answers" in the backs of their books (starting on p. 113).

2. Make sure the arrangements for refreshments (if you're planning to have them) are covered.

3. If your group has decided to use a prayer list, make sure this is covered.

4. If a new couple joins the group for the first time this session, you will want to be sure to introduce them to the other couples. Also, during Warm-Up let them introduce themselves to the group by sharing how and when they met. You should also recap the main points from Session One and have couples record contact information in their books (p. 14).

5. Remember the importance of starting and ending on time.

6. If you told the group during the first session that you'd be asking them to share something they learned from the first HomeBuilders Project, be sure to ask them. This is an opportunity to establish an environment of accountability. However, be prepared to share a personal example of your own.

7. Question 6 in Blueprints calls for couples to look up different Scripture passages. This approach allows for the group to simultaneously examine multiple passages. This saves time and gives the group a chance to learn from one another.

8. Blueprints question 12 in this session gives people in the group the opportunity to share how they came to understand the love of God through Christ. You may want to think of people in the group who you know would be comfortable answering this question and ask them ahead of time to be prepared to share what God has done in their lives.

9. For the closing prayer in this session, you may want to ask for a volunteer or two to close the group in prayer. Check ahead of time with a couple of people you think might be comfortable praying aloud.

Commentary

Note: The numbers that follow correspond to the Blueprints questions of the same numbers in the session.

6. *Exodus 15:11:* This passage speaks of God's power to do anything, and it also mentions his holiness. Because God is perfectly holy, it is impossible to be in his presence unless our sins have been washed clean.

Psalm 24:8-9: The mightiness of God is important for children to remember when they feel helpless and fearful.

Psalm 33:6-11: Our proper response is to fear God. In our culture today, children are taught that we are here merely by chance. It's important for them to know that there is a God who created us and who has ultimate control.

Psalm 139:1-4: This is the foundation for teaching our children that we are accountable to God for our thoughts, words, actions, and attitudes.

Lamentations 3:22-23: God is steadfast and faithful, even when we are not. We can trust God completely.

1 John 4:8-10: Because God is love, we are to show his love to others. That should set us apart in an unbelieving world.

7. Amazingly, this all-powerful, all-knowing God whom we are studying does not want to be separated from us. God offers us the opportunity to have a special relationship—one that is characterized by love, fulfillment, and purpose.

8. We are separated from and are unable to enjoy a relationship with God because of our desire to please ourselves and our refusal to obey God's commands. This is what the Bible calls sin.

Because God is holy, this sin creates a barrier that keeps us from God.

10. God sent Jesus Christ to pay the penalty for our sin.

11. We need to receive the gift God offers by accepting the invitation to believe in Christ and enter into a personal relationship with Jesus.

Session Three:
Helping Your Children Walk With God

Objectives

Children need to learn from your example and teaching what it means to walk with God.

In this session, parents will...

- talk about what their children need to know to walk with Christ.

- discuss how to make their homes a "spiritual greenhouse" where children can discover how to walk with God.

- identify practical, everyday ways to pass on scriptural truths to their children.

- share stories about how God has worked in their lives— stories they can also tell their children.

Notes and Tips

1. Congratulations! With the completion of this session, you will be halfway through this study. It's time for a checkup: How are you feeling? How is the group going? What has worked well so far? What things might you consider changing as you head into the second half?

2. For the Warm-Up in this session, parents are given the opportunity to write a parenting question and a prayer request that will be shared with the group. You will need to have index cards (two per person) or pieces of paper available. Group members will give you their questions and requests. Read as many of the question cards as you have time for during Warm-Up, and plan to read as many of the prayer request cards as you have time for during this session's closing prayer time. You may only have time for a card or two. That's OK. Keep these cards and incorporate them, a card or two at a time, in future sessions (as part of either the Warm-Up or closing prayer time).

3. **For Extra Impact:** An alternate idea for this session's Warm-Up is an exercise called *Tell and Show*. If you decide to do this activity, you will need to put together a basket, bucket, or bowl full of various kitchen utensils or tools—a fork, spoon, spatula, can opener, hammer, pliers, and screw driver, for example. Instruct each person in the group to select at least one tool or utensil. Then have everyone think about a task that utilizes the instrument he or she selected but that a child might not understand how to carry out properly or safely without being shown how. (For example, you can tell a child how to hold a fork while eating, but he or she may not understand unless you domonstrate how to hold a fork.) Have everyone share the task they thought of.

4. You may find it helpful to make some notes right after the meeting to help you evaluate how this session went. Ask yourself questions such as: Did everyone participate? Is there anyone I need to make a special effort to follow up with before the next session? Asking yourself questions like these will help you stay focused.

Commentary

Note: The numbers that follow correspond to the Blueprints questions of the same numbers in the session.

2. Many Christians would say that the duty of a Christian is to pray, study the Bible, and worship God. However, the real essence of the Christian life is to love and serve God and others.

4. The home is the primary place where the character and values of children are shaped. Children are influenced by other people and by our culture, but nothing matches the daily impact of the family. This is where we have the best chance to teach children about God and also model to them on a daily basis what it means to walk with him.

5. This passage shows us that we should tell our children about God's Word on a daily basis, as a part of everyday life, "when you sit at home and when you walk along the road, when you lie down and when you get up."

A follow-up question you could ask is: What are some everyday opportunities you could use to teach God's Word to your children?

6. If children learn Scripture from their parents but the parents do not live out those truths, the children may grow up believing that the Bible is little more than a collection of commands that cannot be followed in everyday life.

7. If biblical principles are modeled but not taught, children may well emulate the behavior of their parents but may also conclude that there is little need for God.

10. People remember stories—hearing how God is working in your life will provide inspiration. These stories will serve as examples of what God could do in their own lives and may help give them the strength and determination to trust God in similar circumstances in the future.

Session Four:
Building Character in Your Children

Objectives

Just as your children need training in everyday living skills, they also need training in character.

In this session, parents will...

- learn a practical definition for *character*.
- discuss why children need training in character.
- examine key principles for character training.

Notes and Tips

1. You and your spouse may want to write notes of thanks and encouragement to the couples in your group this week. Thank them for their commitment and contribution to the group, and let them know that you are praying for them. (Make a point to pray for them as you write their notes.)

2. As you come to the end of the discussion for the Wrap-Up, you may want to share the following note from the authors: "We faced a similar situation with a child, and here's what we did: We met with the child to review the situation. We said that he needed to keep control over his emotions and that if he did not, we would not allow him to continue competing. Soon afterward he was competing in a tournament that he probably would have won. But the unacceptable behavior began again, and Dennis ended up walking onto the court in the middle of a match our son was winning. 'This match is over,' he said and led our son off the court."

3. If you still have parenting questions or special prayer requests from the Session Three Warm-Up activity, address as many as you have time for during either Warm-Up or the closing prayer time.

4. By this time, group members should be getting more comfortable with one another. For prayer at the end of this session, you may want to give everyone an opportunity to pray by asking the group to finish a sentence that goes something like this: "Lord, I want to thank you for..." Be sensitive to anyone who may not feel comfortable doing this.

Commentary

6. Depending on the size of your group and how you are doing on time, you may want to have couples or groups of couples each look up one of the three passages to read and discuss in relation to the question. Then each group could report its insights. This approach can help to engage people and save time.

Note: The numbers that follow correspond to the Blueprints questions of the same numbers in the session.

8. Examples can include sending a child to his room for a specified time; depriving the child of something he desires, such as dessert, allowance, television, computer, or a trip to a ballgame; assigning extra chores; setting up a plan for making restitution to someone who has been affected by the child's actions; "grounding" the child from outside activities for a period of time; and spanking. Evaluate what form of punishment is appropriate for the age of your child. Try to determine punishment ahead of offenses, and make an effort to make the punishment fit the crime. Just as some parents fail to institute any discipline at all, others go overboard and punish too harshly for relatively minor offenses.

In discussing the topic of discipline, be sensitive to the possibility that not everyone in the group agrees about what is appropriate. Allow for a positive exchange, but be prepared to move on and keep the session on track. While discipline is an important subject, it is just one component of building character, which is what's being studied in this session. For a more in-depth look at the topic of discipline from a biblical perspective, the group may be interested in planning to study another HomeBuilders Parenting Series course, *Establishing Effective Discipline for Your Children*, in the future.

9. It can be deceptively easy for a parent to slip into a critical mode, emphasizing correction and discipline over praise. Being aware of this tendency is one step toward avoiding it.

A possible follow-up question to use is, What are some specific ways you have praised, encouraged, or rewarded your children's good behavior that have been effective in your home?

Session Five:

Training Your Children to Love Others

Objectives

Children need to learn what it means to "love your neighbor as yourself."

In this session, parents will...

- explore the meaning of the "Greatest Commandment."

- focus on practical ways they can train their children to love others.

- discuss the need for humility and respect in relationships.

- discover key principles to teach children about resolving conflict.

Notes and Tips

1. The home is the best place for children to learn how to build and maintain good relationships with others. Every day, as they interact with parents and siblings, they have opportunities to practice what it means to love others. This session will help parents think of practical ways to take advantage of this environment.

2. For question 6, depending on the size of your group, you may want to break into subgroups if you haven't already done so. Have the groups create their lists and then come back together and compare.

You may want to provide separate sheets of paper for the groups to list the principles they find. Or, if available to you, use flip charts, white boards, or newsprint and markers.

3. If you still have parenting questions or special prayer requests, be sure to address as many as you have time for.

Commentary

Note: The numbers that follow correspond to the Blueprints questions of the same numbers in the session.

1. Children, just like adults, are naturally selfish. Children may show kindness and compassion in one circumstance and spitefulness or cruelty in another.

Related follow-up questions you may want to ask in conjunction with this question are, "What is the natural tendency of children in relationships?" and "How do they act toward other people?"

6. Some of the principles are "be devoted to one another"; "honor others above yourself"; "share what you have with those who are in need"; "practice hospitality"; "don't seek revenge, but bless those who persecute and curse you"; "live at peace with everyone"; and "show compassion to the needy."

8. A possible follow-up question: What does pride do to relationships?

Session Six:
Imparting a Sense of Purpose

Objectives

As parents, we need to raise our children with the knowledge that they will be released to a life of mission and purpose.

In this session, parents will...

- share how they have benefited from participating in this study.
- study the process of "releasing" a child into greater responsibility as he or she matures.
- examine biblical priorities for our purpose in life.

Notes and Tips

1. This final session of the study reminds parents that children will not be living at home all their lives. Parents need to raise children knowing that someday they will live on their own.

In the opening session, parents were challenged to think of the type of people they wanted their children to become. This session returns to this topic by challenging parents to consider whether their goals for their children line up with biblical priorities.

2. For the Warm-Up, you may want to provide separate sheets of paper or, if available, a flip chart, white board, or newsprint and markers for the list the group will create.

3. For Extra Impact: Here's a suggestion for making the closing prayer time of this final session special. Have the group form a prayer circle. Then have each couple or person, if comfortable doing so, take a turn standing or kneeling in the middle of the circle with the group praying specifically for that couple or person. Pray that God will give them wisdom as they raise their children and that he will give them special insight into how they can improve their parenting skills. Also, pray for their children—that they will grow to walk with God.

4. If you still have parenting questions or special prayer requests, be sure to allow time to address these in this session.

5. While this HomeBuilders study has great value, people are likely to return to previous patterns of living unless they commit to a plan for carrying on the progress made. During this final session of the course, encourage couples to take specific steps beyond this study to continue to build their homes. For example, you may want to challenge couples who have developed the habit of a "date night" during the course of this study to continue this practice. Also, you may want the group to consider doing another HomeBuilders study.

6. As a part of this last session, you may want to consider devoting some time to plan for one more meeting—a party to celebrate the completion of this study!

Commentary

3. Release points for children include events such as children feeding themselves, walking unassisted, using the toilet alone, going to school for the first time, earning an allowance, staying overnight with a friend, puberty, being able to choose their own entertainment, permission to use the Internet, choosing their own clothing, attending group functions with members of the opposite sex, dating, driving, later curfews, college, and marriage.

Note: The numbers that follow correspond to the Blueprints questions of the same numbers in the session.

6. In this passage, Paul says his purpose is to help others grow in their progress and joy in the faith. He is more concerned about the needs of others than his own.

7. This command to "make disciples" is directed to every Christian, not just to the disciples who were present to hear Christ's words. This speaks of a purpose and cause greater than ourselves.

8. People today need Christ as much as ever. They may not acknowledge this, but when something tragic happens, many recognize that something is missing in their lives without God.

10. Sometimes we as parents may hinder our children from going out into the world and making an impact for Christ. It may be that we fear for their safety or desire to keep them close and "well-off," as opposed to releasing them and letting them possibly face harsh or poor living conditions in the role of a missionary, for example.

Recommended Resources

Audio Series (available from FamilyLife, 1-800-FL-TODAY)

"How Children Come to Faith in Christ," with Jim Elliff

"Principles for Effective Parenting," with Dennis and Barbara Rainey

Bible Curriculum

FaithWeaver™ Bible Curriculum (available from Group Publishing, Inc.)

Books

A Mother's Heart, by Jean Fleming

Different Children, Different Needs, by Charles F. Boyd

Dr. James Dobson on Parenting: Includes *The Strong-Willed Child & Parenting Isn't for Cowards*, by Dr. James Dobson

Family Matters, by Kyle and Sharon Dodd

Fathers & Sons, by Ron and Matt Jenson

Fun Excuses to Talk About God, by Joani Schultz (available from Group Publishing, Inc.)

Home by Choice, by Brenda Hunter

How to Lead a Child to Christ, by Daniel H. Smith

How to Really Love Your Child and *How to Really Love Your Teenager*, by Ross Campbell

The New Dare to Discipline, by Dr. James Dobson

Parenting Today's Adolescent, by Dennis and Barbara Rainey

Parenting Without Pressure, by Teresa A. Langston

Real Family Values, by Robert Lewis and Rich Campbell

Shepherding a Child's Heart, by Ted Tripp

Tender Warrior, by Stu Weber

Watchmen on the Walls, by Anne Arkins and Gary Harrell

What Really Matters at Home, by John and Susan Yates

Prayer Requests

Prayer Requests

Prayer Requests

Prayer Requests

Does Your Church Offer Marriage Insurance?

Great marriages don't just happen—husbands and wives need to nurture them. They need to make their marriage relationship a priority.

That's where the HomeBuilders Couples Series® can help! The series consists of interactive 6- to 7-week small group studies that make it easy for couples to really open up with each other. The result is fun, non-threatening interactions that build stronger Christ-centered relationships between spouses—and with other couples!

Whether you've been married for years or are newly married, this series will help you and your spouse discover timeless principles from God's Word that you can apply to your marriage and make it the best it can be!

The HomeBuilders Leader Guide gives you all the information and encouragement you need to start and lead a dynamic HomeBuilders small group.

The HomeBuilders Couples Series includes these life-changing studies:

- Building Teamwork in Your Marriage
- Building Your Marriage *(also available in Spanish!)*
- Building Your Mate's Self-Esteem
- Growing Together in Christ
- Improving Communication in Your Marriage *(also available in Spanish!)*
- Making Your Remarriage Last
- Mastering Money in Your Marriage
- Overcoming Stress in Your Marriage
- Resolving Conflict in Your Marriage

And check out the HomeBuilders Parenting Series!

- Building Character in Your Children
- Establishing Effective Discipline for Your Children
- Guiding Your Teenagers
- Helping Your Children Know God
- Improving Your Parenting
- Raising Children of Faith

Look for the **HomeBuilders Couples Series and HomeBuilders Parenting Series** at your favorite Christian supplier or write:

Bringing Timeless Principles Home

www.familylife.com

P.O. Box 485, Loveland, CO 80539-0485.
www.grouppublishing.com

$\mathbb{F}$ amilyLife has been presenting couples with the wonderful news of God's blueprints for marriage since 1976. Today we are strengthening hundreds of thousands of homes each year in the United States and around the world through:

- ◆ **Weekend to Remember** conferences

- ◆ **One-day arena events** for couples

- ◆ **HomeBuilders Couples Series®** and **HomeBuilders Parenting Series®** small-group Bible studies

- ◆ **"FamilyLife Today,"** the daily, half-hour radio program, and four other nationally syndicated broadcasts

- ◆ A comprehensive Web site, **www.familylife.com**, featuring marriage and parenting tips, daily devotions, conference information, and a wide range of resources for strengthening families

- ◆ Unique marriage and family **connecting resources**

Through these outreaches, FamilyLife is effectively developing godly families who reach the world one home at a time.

FAMILYLIFE™
Bringing Timeless Principles Home

Dennis Rainey, President
1-800-FL-TODAY (358-6329)
www.familylife.com
A division of Campus Crusade for Christ